CELEBRATING

THE

UNIVERSE!

ALSO BY JAMES MULLANEY

The Cambridge Double Star Atlas
(Cambridge University Press)

The Cambridge Atlas of Herschel Objects
(Cambridge University Press)

Edgar Cayce and the Cosmos (A.R.E. Press)

Double and Multiple Stars and How to Observe Them
(Springer-Verlag)

The Herschel Objects and How to Observe Them
(Springer-Verlag)

A Buyer's and User's Guide to Astronomical Telescopes &
Binoculars (Springer-Verlag)

Celestial Harvest: 300-Plus Showpieces of the Heavens for
Telescope Viewing and Contemplation (Dover)

The Finest Deep-Sky Objects (Sky Publishing)

CELEBRATING

THE

UNIVERSE!

THE SPIRITUALITY & SCIENCE
OF STARGAZING

JAMES MULLANEY

Fellow of the Royal Astronomical
Society of London

HAY HOUSE, INC.
Carlsbad, California • New York City
London • Sydney • Johannesburg
Vancouver • Hong Kong • New Delhi

Published and distributed in the United States by: Hay House, Inc.:
www.hayhouse.com • *Published and distributed in Australia by:*
Hay House Australia Pty. Ltd.: www.hayhouse.com.au • *Published
and distributed in the United Kingdom by:* Hay House UK, Ltd.:
www.hayhouse.co.uk • *Published and distributed in the Republic
of South Africa by:* Hay House SA (Pty), Ltd.: www.hayhouse.co.za
• *Distributed in Canada by:* Raincoast: www.raincoast.com • *Published in India by:* Hay House Publishers India: www.hayhouse.co.in

Cover design: Angela Moody | amoodycover.com
Interior design: Tricia Breidenthal
Cover image of the Helix Nebula: NASA, NOAO, ESA, the Hubble Helix
Nebula Team, M. Meixner (STScI), and T.A. Rector (NRAO)

Library of Congress Cataloging-in-Publication Data

Mullaney, James.
   Celebrating the universe! : the spirituality & science of stargazing /
James Mullaney, Fellow of the Royal Astronomical Society of London.
-- 1st edition.
      pages cm
   ISBN 978-1-4019-4172-7 (pbk.)
   1. Stars--Observations--Miscellanea. I. Title.
   QB801.M85 2013
   201'.652--dc23

                                             2013003530

ISBN: 978-1-4019-4172-7

16   15   14   13   4   3   2   1
1st edition, June 2013

FSC
MIX
Paper
FSC® C011935

. . . .

To my wonderful wife,
Sharon McDonald Mullaney . . .
whose love and support
made it all possible.

. . . .

CONTENTS

PART IV: WONDERS OF DEEP SPACE

INTRODUCTION

Genesis & Purpose of This Celestial Travel Guide

You are holding in your hands your personal passport to the stars! *And there has never been one like it before.*

It's estimated that some ten million people in the U.S. alone possess telescopes, plus countless others who own binoculars and spotting scopes—all of which can be turned to viewing the night sky. And there are plenty of handbooks on how and what to look at overhead. But until now, *none* of these have been based on the metaphysical and spiritual aspects of communing with the heavens, which may well be the greatest value that looking at the stars offers the individual. (Among these aspects are therapeutic relaxation, celestial meditation, expansion of consciousness, spiritual contact, and astral travel.) As such, these previous guides have overlooked the very soul of the night! In writing this book for you, I will have hopefully filled this long-standing need at last.

Star lovers around the world are all in agreement on one thing: *there is something inherently spiritual about looking up at the night sky!* Perhaps you've experienced such feelings yourself—for example, when you went outdoors on a clear, cold winter's night and beheld the awesome spectacle of Orion and all the radiant gems gracing the sky at that time of the year.

This is first and foremost a spiritual guide to the heavens, intended to greatly enhance such uplifting and inspiring feelings by introducing you to the sky's many wonders—both physical and metaphysical.

A Majestic Approach

Throughout this "travel guide," I will be pointing out the many exciting celestial objects and events to be seen in the sky, along with the basic astronomy associated with them so that you may fully understand and appreciate what it is that you're seeing. Just as tourists in foreign lands get much more out of their travels by knowing something beforehand about the places they visit, so too do "travelers" exploring the heavens. But the overriding emphasis will be on the beauty and grandeur and, yes, the *spirituality* of the scenes before you—what might be called the "poetry" of the stars, rather than just cold, impersonal facts about them. As noted comet discoverer David Levy put it, "I became an astronomer not to learn the facts about the sky but to feel its majesty."

You and I have come together to celebrate the universe, which rewards star lovers with priceless moments of sublime beauty and tranquility. I'm personally a hopeless "romantic" in my approach to astronomy. Although I worked for a number of years in the professional side of the field, it's always been its aesthetic and spiritual aspects that have so turned me on to it. Even die-hard researchers have admitted to me that astronomy loses half its meaning by overlooking its "soft side," as it's often referred to—or as one of them put it, by forgetting to pursue astronomy with "an uncovered head and humble heart."

I confess that I've had a lifelong love affair with the universe. And yes, I'm convinced that it loves me in return!

What Is Stargazing?

Let's begin by defining *stargazing*. Quite simply, it's the sheer joy of seeing firsthand the wonders of the heavens. No astrophysics, cosmology, celestial mechanics, or mathematics involved or needed here! It's surely the next best thing to actually being "out there" yourself in space.

Over the years, stargazing has been variously described—by individuals ranging from novice skywatchers to seasoned astronauts—as:

- A space-age hobby
- The ultimate trip
- A mind-expanding cosmic journey
- An exhilarating ride
- A fraternity of the mind chartered at the dawn of time
- A spiritual pilgrimage
- The great escape
- A magic carpet to the stars

And those of us who pursue it have been called:

- Star hustlers
- Naturalists of the night
- Time travelers
- Harvesters of starlight
- Star pilgrims
- Citizens of heaven

This only hints at the heady excitement that awaits you when you attend the nightly sky show overhead. As the Sun sets on clear evenings, pulling back the blanket of night over the Earth and many of its inhabitants, a drama of cosmic proportions unfolds. The cast of characters includes the brightest luminaries of the celestial stage, all assembled for your personal enjoyment. You have a front-row seat. And the cost is absolutely free!

Yet most of humanity prefers to stay indoors fixated before television and computer screens. Only the star lovers are awake to the majesty that unfolds once darkness falls. Indeed, many of us feel that stargazing is a sacred privilege bestowed on those who choose to "reach for the sky."

A Taste of Celestial Glory

There's indeed much to see in the sky with just the unaided eye alone, and this will be the emphasis throughout the upcoming chapters. One of life's great treasures is simply looking up on a clear night and seeing the stars and constellations blaze forth in mystical splendor in the vault of heaven. But given the assistance of even a humble pair of binoculars or small telescope, an entire unsuspected universe awaits your inspection!

Imagine yourself peering through the porthole of one of these optical "spaceships" at sights like the following:

- The majestic mountains, craters, and valleys of the Moon's alien surface

- The changing phases of dazzling Venus

- The seasonal melting of the Martian polar caps, and its blue-green-splotched orange deserts

- Jupiter's colorful cloud belts and four jewel-like bright satellites dancing nightly to and fro about the giant planet

- The incredibly breathtaking ice rings of Saturn

- The green and blue remote outer worlds of Uranus and Neptune, respectively

- A newly discovered comet rushing sunward and sprouting a long scimitar-like tail

And our solar system is but a drop in the cosmic ocean. Far out in the depths of interstellar space are:

- Exquisitely tinted, waltzing double- and multiple-star systems

- Fiery pulsating supergiant suns

- Glittering star clusters—the stellar jewel boxes and beehives of the cosmos

- Glowing clouds of hydrogen gas incubating new stars and their planets

- The magnificent massed star clouds of our Milky Way Galaxy

And finally, out in the great beyond, are the other galaxies themselves—"island universes" containing billions of stars so remote that their light takes millions of years or more just to reach us.

Happily, and perhaps surprisingly to many of those beginning in this wonderful pastime, despite their great distances from us, representatives of all of these various deep-space marvels can actually be seen *without any optical assistance at all*—including galaxies! A universe of wonders awaits those who would simply take time to learn what to see and where to look in its great expanse.

In the Presence of the Original

There's another, less obvious, exciting aspect of stargazing that should be pointed out here.

The original masterworks of the heavens are <u>yours</u> *to see and enjoy, as much accessible to you as to the great observatories of the world!*

I have yet to meet the amateur fossil collector who boasts having a complete dinosaur skeleton in his possession, or the budding nuclear physicist who has a cyclotron in her basement and is studying the various parts of the atom. In contrast, the backyard observer has access to virtually every major class of celestial object *in its pure and original form*—not simply in a photograph, but visible to the eye—from the Moon and planets to galaxies and quasars.

And as has often been pointed out, there is no privilege like that of standing in the presence of the original. Just compare, for example, looking at a print of a famous painting to actually seeing the work in person at a museum. (Andrew Wyeth's *Christina's World* comes to mind; to me, the countless reproductions in circulation pale in comparison with the original that hangs in the Museum of Modern Art.)

I will have much more to say about this in Chapter 3, especially regarding the phenomenon of the amazing "photon connection." But mentioning a museum here reminds me of how the famed Princeton theoretical physicist John Archibald Wheeler (a colleague of Einstein, and the person who coined the term *black hole*) referred to the universe as "our museum of wonder and beauty, our cathedral."

And so it is to countless numbers of stargazers around the planet, as they wander "starry-eyed" and in awe through the magnificent corridors of creation.

Our Itinerary

This book is divided into four main sections:

— In **Part I: Spiritual Reflections for Your Cosmic Journey**, we explore such provocative and mind-expanding topics as cosmology and the big bang, an expanding/accelerating universe, dark matter and dark energy, other bubble universes beyond ours, faster-than-light travel, and God and the Cosmic Mind. Perhaps most profound of all is the discussion of our heritage as children of the stars (we're made of stardust!) and destiny as citizens of the universe (joining the awaiting galactic community!).

— Then in **Part II: Preparing for Your Cosmic Journey**, you will be equipped with everything you need to know before venturing out under the night sky. This includes valuable tips on the selection and use of binoculars and telescopes.

— **Part III: Wonders of the Solar System** surveys the many marvels right in our own cosmic "backyard," ranging from the Sun and Moon to the planets and comets.

— We finally travel into the "great beyond" in **Part IV: Wonders of Deep Space.** Here we encounter nature at its grandest—from fantastic varieties of individual and groups of stars to entire systems pinnacled in the galaxies themselves. We also examine the eerily beautiful nebulae—those clouds of hydrogen gas that serve as both nurseries at the beginning of a star's life and as crypts at its spectacular end.

My recommendation is that you read this guide cover to cover initially (hopefully finding it a fascinating and easy read!), then go back and review various chapters in Part III and Part IV relating to particular objects you wish to observe on a given night (constellations, the Moon, planets, galaxies, and so on). It will also be helpful to keep in mind the various metaphysical and spiritual benefits you can expect, covered in Part I, as well as the observing hints given in Part II on using the unaided eye, binoculars, and/or a small telescope should you have one. (You may find cloudy nights a good time to reread Parts I and II.)

Note especially the various meditation-related exercises scattered throughout this book. As I discuss in Chapter 3, meditation is the perfect complement to stargazing, so these techniques are worth reviewing (and practicing!) over and over again, as this guide accompanies you on your journey into the vastness of space and time. And even if you don't have access to a telescope to view some of the harder-to-see deep-space wonders featured in Part IV, I invite you to contemplate their grandeur with your "mind's eye" during the "Meditative Moment" interludes throughout this section of the book. I've also quoted many luminaries in the various chapters and would suggest you jot down in a journal any of their words that strike a chord in you and consider reflecting on their profound insights into the cosmos while actually observing it.

Throughout this book I will be sharing personal stories based on a lifetime of introducing the wonders of the heavens to others in my various roles as both an amateur and professional astronomer, as a planetarium and college educator, and as a public speaker. (I actually gave my first public lecture and published my first article both at the age of 12. Now, nearly a thousand articles and nine books later, I'm still at it!) Some of these experiences are quite humorous, while others are truly touching. All serve the purpose of not only illustrating and reinforcing various topics covered but also of, hopefully, making this guide to the spirituality and science of stargazing as pertinent and fascinating to you as possible.

Closing here on a personal note, I've spent more than 50 years as an avid stargazer exploring the highways and byways of the cosmos. And yet I can go out on any clear night and find celestial treasures that I've never seen before—and in so doing, experience awe and spiritual upliftment anew. Our cosmic journey is truly a never-ending one! So I wish you many happy "adventures in starland" as together we venture into the gentle night and . . . *celebrate the universe!*

— **James Mullaney**
Rehoboth Beach, Delaware
Planet Earth

PART I

SPIRITUAL REFLECTIONS FOR YOUR COSMIC JOURNEY

CHAPTER 1

THE BIG BANG & COSMOLOGY

"In the beginning . . ." So start (or words akin to these) the creation accounts from various cultures and faiths and time periods. (Legendary Harvard astronomer Harlow Shapley had his own version: "In the beginning was hydrogen." It's true—primordial hydrogen was the original element from which all others were forged in stellar furnaces.)

It seems appropriate to start off the first chapter of this book by discussing how the universe—everything that we see above our heads, as well as on the Earth—began. And thanks to discoveries in *cosmology* (the scientific study of the origin and history of the cosmos), we now know that there *was* an actual beginning to the universe!

Why is that significant? Well, contrary to what many atheists claim (essentially, that the universe has always been here, and that, as a result, there is no need for a creator-God), there *was* indeed a creation event—and that implies that there was/is a Creator or Creative Force or Prime Mover that started it all. And as I'll discuss, this lends an inherent spirituality to the act of stargazing.

How Did the Universe Begin?

In 1927, Belgian cosmologist and Catholic priest Georges Lemaître first put forth what is now known as the *big bang theory* (no, not the popular TV sitcom of the same name!), which describes that initial event. The British astronomer and cosmologist Fred Hoyle—originator of the continuous-creation theory, discussed in the next section—actually coined the term deridingly since he didn't buy into it. But the big bang is no longer considered just a theory. There's overwhelming observational evidence that it did, in fact, occur. And it happened *13.7 billion years ago.*

Many ask, where did it happen? It happened *everywhere!* All of space and time (or *space-time,* as Einstein called it) were created in the big bang. Contained within the volume of something the size of a green pea (some physicists and cosmologists say the size of a subatomic particle) was all the energy and future matter of today's vast cosmos!

From this colossal event, the universe began expanding outward in all directions, and it's continuing to do so as you read this. All of the galaxies (except those within our Local Group) appear to be rushing away from us. But this doesn't mean that we are at the center of the expanding universe. To understand why, consider the following example. Take a balloon with polka dots all over it and blow it up. As it expands, pick *any* dot as our Milky Way Galaxy. Notice that all the other dots will be seen moving away from it in every direction. However, just as the dot you picked is in no way at the "center" of the balloon's surface, neither is Earth at the center of the universe.

We know the universe is expanding from the "red shifts" in the spectra of light emitted by the galaxies, which show that the farther away they are, the faster they are moving. This is the well-known *Doppler effect,* which is often illustrated using the example of a fire truck rushing toward you. As it approaches, its siren gets higher and higher in pitch since the sound waves emanating from it are being compressed. As it passes you, the pitch immediately drops since the sound waves are now being stretched out. This works the same for light as well: all of the lines in galaxy spectra are shifted from their normal positions to lower frequencies (that is, to the red end of the spectrum)—thus the term *red shift.* A few of the galaxies in our Local Group are actually approaching the Milky Way and do show a "blue shift," as expected.

But there's more to this story! Einstein's equations in theoretical physics showed evidence of an expanding universe even before it was actually observed. However, this great genius refused to accept the expansion as reality and actually introduced a "fudge factor," which he called a *cosmological constant,* to cancel it out—thus keeping the universe static, as he believed it was. After being shown proof later (by astronomers at the Mount Wilson Observatory) that the universe was indeed expanding, he called this his "biggest blunder." There was also evidence in Einstein's work that the universe was not just expanding but accelerating as well!

More than half a century was to pass before astronomers found observational proof that there is actually some kind of an "antigravity" force of a totally unknown nature causing galaxies, and entire galaxy clusters, to rush outward at ever-greater velocities. Indeed, some of them at the limits of today's largest instruments are moving at nearly the speed of light itself! Proving the existence of this mysterious repulsive force is considered one of the greatest triumphs of observational cosmology—one for which the researchers involved received the Nobel Prize in physics. (Strangely, there is actually no prize awarded for astronomy as such itself.)

Continuous Creation

In 1948 Fred Hoyle, together with colleagues Thomas Gold and Hermann Bondi, put forth the revolutionary theory of *continuous creation* (to me, most eloquently articulated in Hoyle's fascinating popular-level book *The Nature of the Universe*). It's also known as the *steady-state theory.* Essentially, they said that as the galaxies move farther away from us and each other into space, new matter in the form of primordial hydrogen fills the void to take their place *from out of nowhere!*

At the time this was considered sheer fantasy. But today with all the discussion of "zero-point energy" and "quantum fluctuations" in the "vacuum" of space, it appears as if Hoyle may have been right after all. (In essence, these terms refer to the fact that apparently space isn't really empty, as we think of it—that quantized pulses of energy are manifesting to create a so-called quantum foam.) As this new energy (and from it, matter) appears, it's replacing that which is lost by the recession of the galaxies—so the overall "density" of the universe remains essentially unchanged.

It looks as though continuous creation and a steady-state universe *are* compatible with an expanding universe. Lemaître and Hoyle were apparently both right!

The Dark Side of the Universe

By now, just about everyone has heard the surprising discovery that most of the universe is invisible to us! And we're not talking about "stuff" out beyond the reach of our existing telescopes—or shining at wavelengths we can't see. (The entire electromagnetic spectrum—from the x-ray and ultraviolet end to the infrared, microwave, and radio one—is now under intense observation by astronomers, both from the ground and from space.) Within the vast bubble we call "our universe," less than 5 percent of it can be detected by any of our instruments. That percentage includes all of the stars and nebulae and galaxies we know. About 20 percent consists of some unidentified strange form of matter, called *dark matter*. We know it's there from the way if affects the universe we can see. Even more amazing is that 75 percent of this invisible universe consists of an unknown mysterious force called *dark energy*. It's the "antigravity" force I mentioned.

Prior to the discovery that the universe is expanding *and* accelerating, cosmologists expected gravity to eventually slow down the expansion and then reverse it—resulting in all of the galaxies rushing back together and ending in a colossal "big crunch" (whereupon another big bang would occur!). But this isn't going to happen, thanks to the repulsive force of dark energy. (Incidentally, there's nothing ominous about the use of the term *dark*. It simply means that the matter and energy are invisible to us.)

I personally find something profoundly spiritual about the concepts of dark matter and dark energy. Perhaps it's the fact that they clearly demonstrate how much of the universe's wonders remain unknown to us. The more we advance in our scientific knowledge of creation, the more we realize how little we actually understand! Cosmology especially makes this so very apparent.

Alice Meynell's profoundly moving 1913 cosmic poem "Christ in the Universe" contains these stanzas reflecting on the mysteries of creation:

> *Nor, in our little day,*
> *May His devices with the heavens be guessed,*
> *His pilgrimage to thread the Milky Way*
> *Or His bestowals there be manifest.*
>
> *But in the eternities,*
> *Doubtless we shall compare together, hear*
> *A million alien Gospels, in what guise*
> *He trod the Pleiades, the Lyre, the Bear.*

I'm sure our Creator (however you perceive or define such a force or being) intended it to be this way. For without the unknown beckoning us, we would cease our explorations. And as Robert Browning so eloquently expressed it: "Ah, but a man's reach should exceed his grasp, / Or what's a heaven for?" I believe that at least part of what heaven is all about is having *all* knowledge made available to the seeker. (And in my view, part of it is also being able to roam the universe in our celestial bodies, as discussed in the next chapter.)

Bubble Universes

If these discoveries aren't mind-blowing enough, there's still more! This vast universe that we're living in—an enormous sphere that stretches some 14 billion light-years in all directions from us—*may be only one of a multitude of other "bubble universes,"* as they are being called. So sure are cosmologists of their existence that they have coined the term *multiverse* to describe the totality of all these separate universes. And just our bubble alone is 28 billion light-years in size. It seems obvious from what's been discussed so far that the universe intends us to be in a constant state of amazement. But now we need to expand that to the *multiverse's* intention!

To be honest with you, the latest discoveries in cosmology (and in the quantum world as well) seem much like *Alice in Wonderland* to this simple stargazer! Yes, I'm amazed—but I also have difficulty comprehending and visualizing these concepts. I imagine you may feel the same.

Fortunately, we're in good company. Even great visionaries like science-fiction author Arthur C. Clarke have had to resort to analogies in order to come to grips with such strange ideas. In the case of bubble universes, he said that they are like the foam on the seashore that washes up with the waves, with the bubbles in the foam repeatedly appearing and then disappearing. As we attempt to process these awesome new discoveries and contemplate their profound implications, Einstein's famous comment that *imagination* is more important than *knowledge* seems appropriate here. The universe provides the star pilgrim with endless exciting opportunities to cultivate both!

So What Does All This Mean to Stargazers?

As we contrast the simple pleasures and joys of stargazing to such heady concepts as dark matter and dark energy, an expanding/accelerating universe, and bubble universes (all of which are part of the utterly amazing universe orchestrated by God/Cosmic Mind/Spirit), we may well wonder if there's a connection between them.

And the answer is yes, there emphatically *is* one! As writer Sherwood Eliot Wirt stated long ago: "What we see though the giant telescopes is an expression of joy by the Creator."

And this in turn goes back to the basic premise that the more we know about the universe that surrounds us, the more admiration we will experience for its Author—and also the more meaning its visual wonders will hold for us. While we can't physically "see" any of the concepts cosmology has brought to light, knowledge of them certainly impacts what we *can* see. Whenever I venture out on a clear night to commune with the sky, I like to peer into the darkness and think about what's happening out there—about stars and planets and galaxies and even entire universes being born and evolving, ever moving and changing.

Stargazing makes each of us a *participant* in the awesome cosmic drama unfolding overhead, both the part of the show that's visible "onstage" and that which is "behind the curtains" and unseen. And as theoretical physicist John Archibald Wheeler pointed out, we're living in a *participatory universe.* This is based on one of the tenets of quantum physics—*that we affect the universe by the very act of observing it!* (This, I know, surely seems to defy everyday human logic and understanding. But just as surely, it appears to be true! It hints at what a profound gap exists between our minds and that of our Creator when it comes to comprehending creation at all its levels.)

Realizing this about our universe brings to mind for me Walt Whitman's comment that he believed "a leaf of grass is no less than the journeywork of the stars." Another favorite line of mine concerning our intimate link on this planet with the cosmos is from playwright Jean Giraudoux: "I know perfectly well that at this very moment the whole universe is listening to us—and that every word we say echoes to the remotest star."

I will have more to say about our amazing connectedness with the universe in the next chapter. But for now, realize what a profound, sacred privilege it is to be a "stargazer." Not only are we witness to the great cosmic play written by a divine hand, but we are also personally participating in its unfolding by the simple act of looking up at the night sky!

In the next chapter we will examine the profound issues of our cosmic destiny as a species and our intimate connection to the Spirit drawing us there. Prepare to be challenged . . . and "wowed"!

CHAPTER 2

OUR COSMIC DESTINY

As mentioned in the Introduction to this celestial travelogue, physically speaking each of us is made of "stardust." Look at your hand and touch one of your fingernails. The calcium it is made of came from inside of a star! So, too, did the carbon forming the cells of your skin. And the iron that's coursing through the blood vessels that are seen just under your skin. Yes, all of the elements in our bodies originally came from the stars.

As Deepak Chopra so beautifully says in his book *The Seven Spiritual Laws of Success,* "We are travelers on a cosmic journey—stardust, swirling and dancing in the eddies and whirlpools of infinity." I, and a great many others I know concerned with the evolution of our species, believe we are ultimately going to return to the stars—to our source—as part of our cosmic destiny! This could be literally in physical form, should we someday discover an easy way to travel to the stars and beyond. But more likely it will occur much sooner, as our planet goes through the "Great Purification" that the Native Americans, among others, feel is coming upon us—essentially, that the living Earth of necessity must periodically "cleanse itself" of toxic life-forms and environmental pollution (especially in the oceans and biosphere), which are endangering it. And it will be the timeless, eternal essence of that which animates us—our soul/spirit—making the transition.

It's quite obvious that we can't roam the universe at will in our physical bodies. But our spirit certainly can! It's widely believed by scientists, philosophers, theologians, and mystics that underlying the material universe we see is an unseen spiritual realm.

The Stargazing Connection

Edgar Cayce (1877–1945) was the famed psychic of Virginia Beach, Virginia, widely known as the "Sleeping Prophet." A majority of his more than 14,000 readings concerned health issues, earning him the title "Father of Holistic Medicine." Many others concerned past lives. But the most fascinating readings to me involve the cosmos (and are the basis for my book *Edgar Cayce and the Cosmos*). In these he talked about us becoming "citizens of the universe" and joining celestial beings on other worlds as our ultimate destiny.

Likewise, the late astronomer and science popularizer Carl Sagan (who was also my friend and mentor) spoke hopefully of us someday becoming part of the "galactic community." Countless classic science-fiction writers have shared the dream of traveling to the stars, and interfacing there with other beings vastly older and wiser than we are. We seem to have a "genetic predisposition" to want to go into space. The noted social writer and "waterfront philosopher" Eric Hoffer called it a *homing impulse* that's drawing us to where we came from. Indeed, when I look at the heavens, I definitely feel what can only be described as a "genetic tugging" calling me upward and homeward!

The lure of stargazing itself takes many forms. One is the opportunity (and privilege) it affords us of seeing firsthand incredibly beautiful and wonderful things in the heavens. Another is the exciting likelihood that others are "out there" among the lights in the sky looking back at us. But perhaps the ultimate thrill of the stargazing experience is one that goes far beyond the basic act of soaking up photons (light) from across the cosmos. It's the realization that we are looking not only at where we came from, but also where we are destined to go.

Communing one-on-one with the heavens is surely the next best thing to actually being out there—something that even many of the astronauts I've talked to, who actually *have* been out there, agree with. And just as surely in my mind, it's also the best way possible to prepare ourselves for that ultimate cosmic adventure!

To Save a World!

Astronomy has long had very valuable and practical aspects to it—from timekeeping and navigation to the expansion of human consciousness. And stargazing, in particular, has a very practical and immensely (perhaps *critically*) important benefit that I haven't yet touched upon. It involves the impact of sharing the wonders of the night sky with others—be they family and friends, or neighbors and total strangers. Doing so could ultimately help save our troubled civilization from self-destruction by providing that "cosmic perspective" that Carl Sagan often talked about so passionately—and without which he feared we would sooner or later destroy ourselves. Every politician, every military leader, every clergyper-son—*everyone,* in fact—needs to see and understand our place in the cosmos to get their priorities straight.

This has never been better expressed than at the 1948 dedication of the famed 200-inch Hale reflecting telescope on Palomar Mountain, outside of San Diego. Raymond Fosdick, then president of the Rockefeller Foundation, said: "Adrift in a cosmos whose shores he cannot even imagine, man spends his energies in fighting with his fellow man over issues which a single look through this telescope would show to be utterly inconsequential."

How true! And I would extend this to *any* telescope, however small and humble it may be. The impact is de-pendent not on the size of the instrument, but on that of the heart of the person who cares enough to share the sky's glory with another fellow traveler aboard our endangered "Spaceship Earth."

Even the simple act of pointing out to others the brighter stars and constellations and planets visible to the unaided eye is a step in the same direction. (And here I'm reminded of Thomas Carlyle's plaint: "Why did not somebody teach me the constellations, and make me at home in the starry heavens, which are always over-head . . . ?") Showing them the Moon, the Pleiades star cluster, or the Andromeda Galaxy, or letting them sweep the expanse of the Milky Way in a pair of binoculars, goes much further. And if you own a telescope, for the ultimate impact let them peer in awe at the moons of Jupiter, the majestic rings of Saturn, the colorful double star Albireo, or the star nursery in the Orion Nebula. It never ceases to amaze me just how many people have *never* looked through a telescope! If you own one, *you* can help remedy that!

In my years of speaking about the joys of stargazing and showing the wonders of the heavens to others, I've had many touching experiences involving their impact upon individuals. Here's just one example from my early days that has stayed with me and which I'd like to share with you.

On a beautifully clear night at a retreat center in upstate New York, I set up my Celestron telescope following the formal lecture (as I always do—weather permitting, of course!) so that the audience could see and experience the "real thing." In near-total darkness, a very elderly lady came hobbling up to the telescope using a cane, and with her hands noticeably shaking, looked into the eyepiece at Saturn.

She then turned to me and said: "Young man, I'm 90 years old. And this is the most incredible night of my entire life."

Wow! Talk about an impact (both upon her *and* me). "A joy that's shared is a joy made double," as the old English proverb reminds us. It's moments like these that have convinced me of the transformative power of stargazing and inspire my life's work.

We're All Connected

It has often been said that the universe, in some sense, "knew that we were coming." There are some 800 physical constants in nature—numerical values governing the universe, such as the speed of light, the charge of an electron, or the force of gravity, most of them subtle and little-known except to specialists like physicists and cosmologists. These constants seem to have been "fine-tuned" so that the physical world and life as we know it could exist. Amazingly, *a minute change in any one of them and we would not be here!* (For more about this, see the wonderful lecture presentation *Everything is Spiritual* by Rob Bell, available on DVD at **www.robbell.com** [click on "Films"].)

The concept known as the *anthropic principle* says that observations of the universe must be compatible with the conscious life that observes it. There are several versions of it, but essentially it means that only in a universe capable of evolving and supporting life will living beings arise who are capable of observing it. And indeed, not only are we here—but being made of "star stuff" means that we *are* the universe contemplating itself! Now just how awesome is that?

In the previous chapter, I mentioned John Archibald Wheeler's notion that we are living in a *participatory universe*. This basically says that we are created by reality, and reality is created by us. In this profound thinker's view, "Physics gives rise to observer-participancy; observer-participancy gives rise to information; and information gives rise to physics," as he explains in his essay "Information, Physics, Quantum: The Search for Links." This draws on the fundamental premise of quantum physics I touched upon before—that we affect the universe by the very act of observing it! (Probably the finest current work about our "quantum connectedness" to each other and the universe is Gregg Braden's superb book *The Divine Matrix,* which I highly recommend for those wishing to probe deeper into these ideas.)

In saying that we're all connected and impact the universe we observe, we not only mean the seven billion of us currently riding on Spaceship Earth—but also the untold numbers of other sentient beings scattered throughout the cosmos! And since all of us are intimately connected, we may well wonder if we are each creating and seeing the same universe.

All of these concepts are certainly mind-expanding (some might even say mind-blowing) to think about. In any case, the bottom line here for stargazers is the implication that in exploring the sights along the glorious highways and byways of the cosmos, we are impacting them in some subtle and mysterious way as we gaze upon them.

The Power of Knowledge

The great astronomer Johannes Kepler once excitedly exclaimed, "O, telescope, instrument of much knowledge, more precious than any scepter, is not he who holds thee in his hands made king and lord of the works of God?" Are there any limits to the wonders and mysteries of creation revealed by our instruments? I think not. Another of my very favorite quotes that beautifully illustrates this comes from an unknown author, who said that "the larger the sphere of our knowledge, the greater the contact of its surface with the infinity of our ignorance."

As to knowledge itself, it's often been said that nature is the greatest book of knowledge—and nature is surely pinnacled in the stars. Edgar Cayce, on the other hand, claimed: THE BEST BOOK IS SELF—a quote that's emblazoned over the entranceway to the amazing library at the Association for Research and Enlightenment in Virginia Beach. (Open to the public as well as to members, it's the second-largest metaphysical library in the world, the largest being at the Vatican in Rome.)

Back in the mid-1800s, at the dedication of one of this country's oldest "temples of the skies"—the Dudley Observatory in Albany, New York—politician and educator Edward Everett stated:

> The great object of all knowledge is to enlarge and purify the soul, to fill the mind with noble contemplations, to furnish a refined pleasure, and to lead our feeble reason from the works of nature up to its great Author and Sustainer. Considering this as the ultimate end of science, no branch of it can surely claim precedence of Astronomy. No other science furnishes such a palpable embodiment of the abstractions which lie at the foundation of our intellectual system; the great ideas of time, and space, and extension, and magnitude, and number, and motion, and power.

This so perfectly describes what stargazing is all about! Little wonder that many who have started out in the hobby at a young age later became professional astronomers. Others have gone into physics or philosophy or even theology. In my case, early in my career I worked for several years in solid-state physics at a major research laboratory in Pittsburgh—keeping astronomy as my avocation (actually, "passion" would better describe it!). One of the amazing pieces of equipment at the lab made it possible to look inside of silicon and other crystal samples through the porthole of a huge darkened vacuum chamber. More than that, I was actually able to "travel" into and through the crystal lattice structure by increasing the energy of the electron-beam probe.

I could not tell the difference between what I was seeing in that microscopic atomic world and the views of the stars through my telescope at night!

In fact, the atom has often been likened to the solar system and molecules to the galaxy (yes, there are differences, to be sure). Perhaps you may have seen the classic black-and-white movie from the '50s entitled *The Incredible Shrinking Man*. The lead character is afflicted with something that makes him become smaller and smaller, eventually disappearing from sight to all those around him. In the final scene, he finds himself standing on an atom and looking up at a "sky" full of "stars" (other atoms). Talk about connectedness—in this case, between the ultra-small and ultra-large physical universe!

God & Cosmic Mind

"The heavens declare the glory of God; and the firmament sheweth his handywork." So states the well-known Psalm 19. Contemplating the wonders of the heavens as a stargazer is to salute the magnificence of God—however you may view the awesome loving, creative, maintaining force behind the cosmos.

Deborah Byrd, executive producer and cohost of the popular internationally syndicated *Earth & Sky* 90-second radio spots, says that "astronomy is good for people's souls." (She also points out that the sky belongs to all of us, and that "it is glorious and it is free.") *Sky & Telescope* magazine senior editor Alan MacRobert says that "stargazing is remarkably steadying for the soul." And 18th-century poet Edward Young even went a step further, claiming that "the soul of man was made to walk the skies."

One of the metaphysical benefits of stargazing discussed in the next chapter is the possibility of spiritual contact. And this is not about religion in the usual sense of the word. It's about the intimate relation between the awesome scenes upon which we gaze and the great Author of their existence. Again, I (and many other amateur and professional astronomers I personally know) have never felt closer to God than during my nightly vigils under the stars. We all seem to share the deep inner belief so beautifully expressed in the lyrics (attributed to Friedrich Schiller) of Beethoven's immortal "Ode to Joy": "Above the starry firmament / A loving Father must dwell."

As John Bahcall, noted Princeton astrophysicist and one of the moving forces behind the creation of the Hubble Space Telescope, pointed out shortly before his death: "Astronomy has an almost mystical appeal." And he also felt that we should pursue it "because it is beautiful and because it is fun." This, from a highly respected, no-nonsense professional.

There have been a number of great thinkers over the years who have asked if the universe we see about us is only a mystical dream of the great Cosmic Mind—and if we are simply "brain cells" of that dreamer. (This reminds me of the story from the Chinese philosopher Zhuangzi, who awakened from a dream about a butterfly, and asked himself: "Am I a man dreaming of a butterfly, or a butterfly dreaming I am a man?")

Cosmically speaking, we're all infants. (And some would say that we act like it much of time, given the "tribal warfare," as Carl Sagan called it, which has characterized our civilization from its very beginning.) We've been here for only a few brief ticks of the cosmic clock. It's hardly to be expected for us to get anything even remotely close to a complete picture of the universe and the Creative Intelligence behind it having so recently come on the celestial scene.

To put this in perspective, it's been calculated that if we were to represent the 4.6-billion-year history of Earth by the height of the Washington Monument in Washington, D.C., *then recorded history as we know it would be represented by the thickness of one postage stamp sitting on top of it!* A related analogy comes from Carl Sagan—one he used and graphically illustrated by a life-size calendar he could actually walk across in his *Cosmos* TV series: if the history of the Earth is represented by the span of one full year, then we humans appear on the scene *in the last 30 seconds of the last day of the year!*

An astronomer (who prefers to remain unidentified) working with some of the world's largest optical telescopes has privately said to a number of his close friends and colleagues: "When we finally look out far enough to see the big bang and that initial spark of creation, we are going to look directly into the face of God." Abraham Lincoln (one of more than a dozen American Presidents who were stargazers, including Thomas Jefferson) also talked about looking into the face of God—in his case by simply staring up at the night sky.

The Intersection of Science & Spirituality

The distinguished late NASA astronomer Robert Jastrow in his book *God and the Astronomers* offers a very revealing metaphor about what the public perceives as the conflict between science and religion. The book talks about scientists, living by their faith in the power of reasoning, having scaled the mountains of ignorance. As they are about to pull themselves over the highest peaks, they are "greeted by a band of theologians who have been sitting there for centuries"!

It seems so very clear to me (as it has seemed to many others) that any "true religion" must be a universal one and not just one focused solely on this "small blue dot," as Carl Sagan called our planet. My God is a big God— that of the entire cosmos! And I think that most will agree that there's a huge difference between religion, as such, and spirituality. *The power behind the universe at all of its levels is inherently spiritual!* Just ask any quantum physicist or astronomer or cosmologist—or even any enlightened theologian.

And as to the perceived conflict between science and religion, I'm reminded that Sagan called for a reconciliation between the two "on the common ground of reverence for the magnificence of the universe." Today, scientists and theologians are actively engaged in a dialogue aimed at just such a reconciliation!

I find it fascinating that the Catholic Church (among other faiths) is now embracing a God of the universe.

This is largely due to the influence of Pope John Paul II, who had a deep interest in astronomy from the age of 11 and who commissioned the Vatican Advanced Technology Telescope at the Mount Graham International Observatory in Arizona. Staffed by Jesuit astronomers, this state-of-the-art instrument is widely referred to as the "Pope Scope." In October of 2000, a Vatican spokesman made the statement that "it is both illogical and arrogant to believe we are the only intelligent beings in God's creation." Then, in the summer of 2005, the Vatican Observatory's headquarters at Castel Gondalfo sponsored an international conference on the topic of "The Search for Life on Other Worlds."

But there's been a long history of church-related remarks about other worlds, most notably this one by 16th-century philosopher, astronomer, and mystic Giordano Bruno: "He is glorified not in one, but in countless Suns; not a single Earth, a single world, but in a thousand thousand, I say in an infinity of worlds."

And then there's Father Pietro Angelo Secchi, the great 19th-century Jesuit astronomer, who went even further. He asked:

> Could it be that God populated only one tiny speck in this cosmos with spiritual beings? It would seem absurd to find nothing but uninhabited deserts in these limitless regions. No! These worlds are bound to be populated by creatures capable of recognizing, honoring and loving their Creator.

Here, I want to relate another personal story. In my lectures to churches and spiritual retreats, I always ask: "What do you plan to do for all eternity once you finally get to heaven?" (This question always ruffles a few feathers!) I then share my personal belief that part of what heaven is all about is roaming God's awesome universe in our spiritual bodies—being anywhere instantly at the speed of thought.

At one evening lecture, a priest was sitting in the front row and staring right in my face. He wasn't the pastor, but just someone who came to hear me, a "celestial evangelist," speak. When I mentioned my belief about heaven, his eyes popped wide open—and I thought, *I'm in big trouble here. He obviously doesn't "buy it."*

Following the lecture, we all went outside to view the Moon and Jupiter through my telescope. He came to the eyepiece to look several times but never said a word to me. The next morning, though, when I turned on my computer, there was an e-mail with a glaring all-caps header that read: **WOW!!!**

It was the "skeptic" priest! He said in all his years as a man of the cloth he had never thought about this possibility—but that he had been up all night thinking about it following the lecture. A year later, I received a message from him telling me that his dearest friend, a fellow priest and his spiritual mentor, had "passed over to be with the Lord." He then went on to say: "I now look forward to gazing upon the wonders of creation in our glorified new bodies with my dear friend. It's going to be quite a show." He obviously *had* bought into the idea, after all . . . and I hope you will as well!

I'm sharing all I've covered in this chapter with you as a fellow stargazer for a couple of reasons:

- First, it reinforces the likelihood—no, the *certainty*—that we are not alone in the universe. As you look out at it, you are seeing a bio-cosmos populated by other intelligent beings! This definitely adds an element of excitement to stargazing beyond that of seeing incredibly wonderful and beautiful things.

- Second, I hope that you'll realize that not only did you come from that universe you're looking at, but that you are destined to return to it and soar about it at will someday.

- Finally, as you experience feelings of spiritual upliftment while stargazing (which you will—again, you're looking at a spiritual universe!), I hope that you'll cherish and nurture whatever form that takes. Realize that the God of all creation is silently communing with you in the glorious Temple of the Skies!

A Higher Destiny

There seems little doubt that humanity has a higher destiny than to remain inhabitants of Spaceship Earth alone. The Russian space pioneer Konstantin Tsiolkovsky said: "Earth is the cradle of humanity, but one cannot live in the cradle forever." (Interestingly, Tsiolkovsky considered himself a "citizen of the universe.") He was almost certainly talking about us moving out into space and exploring it in a physical sense. But his words could also apply to the spiritual realm as well. As one unidentified sage put it: "I'm a child of Earth and starry heaven, but my race is of heaven alone."

There's a realm where the stars are spread out before us like islands basking in the sunlight on the infinite ocean of space. It's a place like the one English poet, novelist, and playwright James Elroy Flecker described a century ago in his poem "The Dying Patriot": ". . . I must go where the fleet of stars is anchored and the young Star-captains glow."

Can't you just picture it? Do you sometimes feel like a "stranger in a strange land" (to use science-fiction master Robert Heinlein's famous line) living here on Earth? I know that I certainly do! Much of the great mass appeal of *Star Trek* is that it takes us to places akin to what Flecker wrote about (as well as provides the optimism that we will overcome our problems on this planet and venture out into the universe as a space-faring race). Being someone who has spent a lifetime as a stargazer, I firmly believe that pursuing our wonderful hobby is the best possible way to prepare ourselves for this ultimate higher destiny. . . .

And so now let's move on to what I consider to be the most profound impact of having a personal and intimate relationship with the heavens: the unsuspected metaphysical joys that stargazing brings.

CHAPTER 3

METAPHYSICAL & SPIRITUAL CONSIDERATIONS

Virtually unknown outside of the field of astronomy itself, the metaphysical and spiritual benefits of stargazing are nevertheless quite real. And they can be experienced even with the unaided eye by anyone who looks up at the sky in contemplative silence on a clear night! Moreover, they typically come as *a complete and joyful surprise* to those just beginning their sky exploration, who may anticipate only the visual thrills and delights the starry heavens offer. But this spiritual dimension of stargazing has a much deeper personal impact than do even the sublime images from space.

Therapeutic Relaxation

Given the state of our stress-filled society today, everyone is seeking ways to relax. Nothing beats stargazing for soothing frayed nerves, tired bodies, and overworked minds—a fact recognized by a growing number of medical practitioners (many of whom as a result have themselves become stargazers!) who treat stress-related illnesses. I've met quite a few therapists at my lectures who regularly "prescribe" some quiet time under the stars for their patients.

Simply staring at a star-filled sky takes the weight of the world off your shoulders. You can literally feel your worries and troubles "evaporating" into the mystical night air. Emerson said that the stars "compose us to a sublime peace." The sky increasingly becomes a sanctuary, your *sanctum sanctorum,* the more time you spend communing with it. There's no question in my mind that the therapeutic benefits of doing so are not only real—but also that they are a priceless gift from Spirit.

Going beyond the basic aspect of therapy for relaxation, there are numerous cases of those whose lives have actually been saved by contact with the tranquility of the heavens. There's one personal experience with this that I would like to share by way of example.

Back in my early college teaching days, I encountered a student who was failing miserably and living in fear of telling her parents. In desperation, she had decided to jump off the roof of one of the classroom buildings. As she was about to get onto the elevator, with tears in her eyes, she saw me entering the lobby for my evening class toting a small telescope. We both went to the roof together. At my invitation, she took one look through the eyepiece—and instantly realized how absurd it was to think about ending her life over grades. (Yes, we had talked on the way up—among other things, I shared with her Mark Twain's quip: "I never let my schooling interfere with my education.")

Fortunately, there's a happy ending to this story. That night, obviously, she elected not to jump. Later on she took my astronomy class, and not only did she ace it but also nearly all of her subsequent courses. During my last contact with her, she was soon to graduate and was thinking about going on to become an astronomer (a third of whom today are women)!

Celestial Meditation

A benefit of stargazing related to therapeutic relaxation is that of celestial meditation. The stars make wonderful "celestial mandalas" upon which to meditate! This is especially true in the case of the brightest luminaries—ones like Sirius in the winter, Arcturus in the spring, Antares in the summer, and Capella in the fall sky—when seen rising over the horizon, at which time glorious prismatic rays flash and dance from their flaming hearts! (Scintillation from atmospheric turbulence near the horizon provides the light show and not actually the stars themselves.)

Here are my suggested steps on just how to try this:

EXERCISE:
Mandala Meditation

- Select a crystal clear night after darkness falls (preferably without the Moon present, which can be a distraction!).

- Either sit comfortably in a folding beach chair or recline on a lawn chair; face east, where stars will be rising as the Earth spins in that direction.

- Examine the horizon for signs of any bright flickering point of light, which will quickly reveal itself to be a star as it slowly rises in the sky.

- Focus your attention on the star as it kaleidoscopically flashes at you. You will be mesmerized—guaranteed!

- If you happen to be nearsighted, for an added treat remove your glasses: the out-of-focus images you see will be even more spectacular! Many find themselves sitting transfixed for hours as they follow the rising of one star after another as our planet slowly spins eastward. (An ocean beach or expansive lake facing east with its smooth horizon makes for an ideal vista to experience this.)

In addition to the real sky, open-eyed meditation can also be done by downloading awesome images from the Hubble Space Telescope onto your computer screen. Of the many thousands available to the public online at Hubble's site (**www.hubblesite.org**), those in its "Gallery" section are the most spectacular and best suited for meditation. Pick a scene that really stirs you, dim the lights, put on some relaxing classical or celestial music—then let your mind soar and your meditation session begin!

Expansion of Consciousness

Staring up at the sky, we're looking into the beginning of everything. We feel young once again, and the child within us is set free. Our minds are opened to receiving, beyond preconceived notions, the most profound insights about creation and the mysteries of the universe.

Some believe that when we're in this contemplative state, we are tapping into the higher-dimensional thoughts of advanced beings communicating with each other telepathically within our Milky Way Galaxy, and even across the universe itself. Indeed, many of the truly great advances in science and technology have come in "flashes of insight" from out of nowhere, according to their discoverers. During a quiet evening of stargazing, don't be surprised if some profound thought or idea flashes through your mind. In some cases it may be from your higher consciousness, while in others (especially if the insight is scientific or technical in nature) from out of the sky. But be alert, as it will typically come and go in an instant!

With most of us using only a very limited percentage of our brain capacity (including geniuses like Einstein!), we might well wonder just what the rest of it is *for*. I'm not alone in being convinced that at least part of that capacity is for telepathic communication, both with each other and also with our celestial neighbors.

One person who shares this view is Apollo 14 astronaut Edgar Mitchell, with whom I had the opportunity to spend three days at a conference we both spoke at several years ago. (What a thrill to shake the hand of a man who has walked on another world!) He conducted documented telepathic experiments while on the Moon's surface with another person back here on Earth—in one instance mentally projecting playing cards randomly and the earthbound receiver calling a high percentage of them correctly! Upon his return, he founded the Institute of Noetic Sciences in California, dedicated to supporting individual and collective transformation through consciousness research. Looking at our beautiful Planet Earth from the Moon was definitely a transformative experience for him!

Spiritual Contact

The elevation of the human spirit through spiritual contact is yet another benefit of stargazing. Virtually every astronomer I've ever met—both amateur and professional—agrees that there's something inherently spiritual about looking up at the night sky. As one of them put it, "Astronomy is a typically monastic activity; it provides food for meditation and strengthens spirituality." And comet discoverer David Levy, whom I quoted in the Introduction, points out: "But aren't silent worship and contemplation the very essence of stargazing?"

Whatever your personal beliefs are about God, the Great Spirit (to use a Native American term), the Cosmic Mind, or the Divine Intelligence behind all of creation, you will come away from your nightly vigils under the stars a holier, more enlightened person as you "worship" in the Temple of the Skies. Your God will become a big God—that of the entire universe and not of just this one small troubled planet.

Observatories themselves are often considered temples by those both who work and visit there. I recall the story of a hard-boiled reporter who was sent to do a magazine feature about the Hale telescope at Palomar. He commented, "A sanctified aura pervades the dome. It seems fitting." (Having been there several times myself, I've had the very same feelings!)

There are those like the great British cosmologist James Jeans, who said that the universe looks more like a great *thought* than like a great machine. (Others say it resembles an epic poem or a grand symphony.) The famed astronomer Johannes Kepler, upon discovering the three laws of planetary motion bearing his name, is reported to have cried out loud: "Oh God, I'm thinking Thy thoughts after Thee!" He obviously realized that he was tapping into the Cosmic Mind from which those laws originated. This means that the spiritual contact we're talking about here may actually entail communing with the God of the Universe directly—rather than through some intermediary, as in conventional religious worship.

On a personal note, I have attended services (and as a speaker presented programs) in churches of many denominations, synagogues, temples, and even ashrams, across the U.S. and abroad. In none of these have I ever experienced the spiritual upliftment that I do under the stars.

This will be a good place to mention that many agnostics and even outright atheists have had spiritual conversions upon seeing the majesty and divine order of the universe. In some cases this has resulted from viewing beautiful celestial images like those from the Hubble

Space Telescope during a lecture, while in others of experiencing the "real thing" through a telescope.

In a related vein, those suffering from various types of addiction have been freed in much the same way—by being shown something of the majestic universe they live in and having some caring person gently point out that the Power behind it all is great enough to heal any addiction. At a retreat facility where I lectured every Saturday afternoon for more than a decade (reaching over 20,000 people annually of all faiths and backgrounds), I had ample opportunity to see this happen firsthand in many lives.

Astral Travel

Perhaps the most sensational metaphysical aspect of stargazing is the possibility of *astral* or *soul travel*. Most of us have heard stories of people who have been out of their bodies (for example, watching oneself driving a car from the backseat!). Their essence—their soul— has briefly traveled elsewhere. Both amateur and professional astronomers have been quietly "coming out of the woodwork" in increasing numbers and sharing their out-of-body experiences that have occurred while observing in their backyards or at remote mountaintop observatories.

We refer to this as "astral" travel since it involves the stars. These events are, without question, real (just ask someone who has had one!). The multitude of documented near-death experiences certainly suggest that something beyond the physical exists inside of us—our astral body or soul—and that it can leave the body. (I've lectured on the same program with noted near-death medical expert Raymond Moody, and have discussed the celestial counterpart of these occurrences with him. We both seem to be describing the same events!) Alone, in the quiet hours of the night, many stargazers have reported being for a few brief moments "out there" among the lights in the sky.

Should this ever happen to you, these prophetic words from Richard Bach's famous novel *Jonathan Livingston Seagull* might hit home: "Perfect speed, my son, is being there." (The implication is that our essence can travel anywhere in the cosmos instantly.) Writer William Fix claims that "our starships are within us" and that "a subtle body that can pass through matter and fly with the speed of thought is indeed a vehicle in which man could cross cosmic distances."

In a later chapter devoted to our Milky Way Galaxy, I'll present a simple procedure by which you, too, may have such an experience. In my more than 20,000 hours of stargazing time logged over the past 50 years, I have astral-traveled on several occasions, and can attest to both the reality of these events and their profound personal impact. They lead to a new, grander view of life and our place in the scheme of things—that "cosmic perspective" that Sagan always talked about and believed was vital to our survival as a species. (I will also have more to say about journeys out of the body in Chapter 8, about the Moon.)

To Touch a Star!

Perhaps astral-travel experiences will be more believable if I share something I've named the *photon connection*. I published the concept formally a number of years ago. Although based on solid scientific fact, its implications have typically been completely overlooked (as in the case of so many such marvels of the universe).

We see stars and galaxies and other celestial objects as a result of the *photons* of light they emit. (In the case of the Moon, planets, and other solar-system members, it's by the light they reflect from the Sun.) And as most people are aware, photons have a strange dualistic nature—they behave like waves and at the same time as particles (or particles traveling in waves, as I prefer to visualize them).

What this means is that when you look at a star, for example, you are getting a piece of something that was once inside of it, which has ended its long journey across space and time on the retina of your eye! *You are in direct physical contact with the star!*

What a privilege it is to actually touch a piece of heaven! The dualistic photons may well be the link that pulls the stargazer out there and back during astral travel, typically all within a matter of seconds. (The truly mind-blowing discovery from quantum physics that it's possible in some cases for a photon *to reach its destination before it has ever left its source* may also be at play here!)

Music of the Spheres

Among others, the well-known psychic Edgar Cayce and astronomer Johannes Kepler, whom I mentioned previously, both talked about "the music of the spheres." This subject is found numerous times in Cayce's readings, a typical example being: "Who may tell a rose to be sweet, or the music of the spheres to harmonize with God?" And Kepler not only claimed to hear this heavenly music, but he also saw celestial harmony in the movement of the planets in their orbits. Similarly, there's the well-known verse in the Book of Job that talks about "when the morning stars sang together."

Some still claim today to hear celestial music while stargazing. And they are not alone. Professional radio astronomers have found evidence of musical notes emanating from certain black holes! (Interestingly, these are B-flat on the musical scale—the same note that soprano and tenor saxophones are tuned to. Perhaps God is a sax player!)

Whether or not you can hear the music of the spheres yourself, you can bring "heavenly harmonies" to your stargazing sessions. Many amateur astronomers I know have space, celestial, or classical music softly playing on headphones while they observe to enhance their visual experiences.

And music is also played at night in many professional observatories, either in the domes themselves or in their control rooms. (These selections often include Holst's famed composition *The Planets,* but I personally prefer something much more soothing. Some of the pieces—especially "Mars"—are anything but relaxing!) A whole genre of space- and celestial-music composers has arisen over the past couple of decades, and their compositions are often heard as background to planetarium presentations as well as being available commercially on CDs. I've listed a few of my favorite albums at the back of the book in Appendix A: Stargazing Resources.

Incidentally, a number of famous astronomers of the past were professional musicians, composers, and/or conductors before turning their attention to the stars—William Herschel (discoverer of the planet Uranus) being one noted example. And conversely, a number of well-known musicians today actually have degrees in astronomy. Lead guitarist Brian May of the British rock band Queen has a Ph.D. in astrophysics and is on the editorial advisory board of *Astronomy* magazine! Music is truly a "universal" language (and I fondly hope within my lifetime to hear alien harmonies beamed to us from the stars!).

Personification of the Stars

Taking the idea that the stars may be singing to us and sending out celestial music a step further, I want to share something that many poets and philosophers have hinted at, something that a growing number of scientists from various fields are suspecting—and something that, if true, means the celestial "cast of characters" entertaining you on clear nights may be more than just a metaphor. The stars in a sense *may actually be "alive"* and not the inanimate objects they've long been thought to be!

In his essay "Nature," the great Emerson said of stars, "every night come out these envoys of beauty, and light the universe with their admonishing smile." Others have talked about them "watching over us as we sleep at night," of them "witnessing all of human history," and of our "looking into their faces." And the English novelist and poet Thomas Hardy wrote: "A star looks down at me / And says: 'Here I and you / Stand, each in our own degree: / What do you mean to do . . . ?'"

Many stargazers (myself included!) find the stars to be "old friends" to whom they can turn time and again for refreshing relief from the worries and pressures of everyday life. And you will, too, as you spend time under the night sky! Seeing majestic Orion, for example, climb up over the eastern horizon in late fall elicits nostalgic emotions and feelings of companionship that are difficult to put into words but which are, nevertheless, quite real.

From a more scientific perspective, a growing number of both astronomers and exobiologists (biologists concerned with the search for extraterrestrial life-forms) have expressed the belief that the dividing line between living and nonliving doesn't occur at our epidermis, nor at the edge of the Earth's atmosphere—but rather at the very edge of the universe itself! The idea of a living universe surrounding us certainly adds an extra dimension of excitement to communing with the stars.

Can the stars, perhaps, "read" thoughts that I send out to them (and which travel instantly across the universe)? Is "wishing upon a star" more than just a lyrical or poetic sentiment?

I've often felt in my nightly vigils under the sky that others out there may be looking back at me. As we will discuss later in this book, the evidence that we are living in a bio-cosmos and that there are other beings on other worlds is simply overwhelming. But then to think that those stars themselves may in some sense have consciousness is even more awe-inspiring (some would say "earth-shattering"). Oh, what an incredible universe we find ourselves in!

Seeing with Mind & Sight

We've now explored here in Part I the all-important spiritual aspects of our cosmic journey. In Part II, we'll next consider the practical preparations necessary before actually embarking on this stargazing adventure. Before we do, there is something very important that must be kept uppermost in your mind—something that connects the preceding discussion with what's to follow.

While some of the visual sights and events in astronomy are quite spectacular (as I'll share in Parts III and IV of this book), many others are very subtle and require "seeing" with more than your vision alone. That dim blur of light barely visible to the eye may be a galaxy containing 500 billion stars!

Or closer to home, let's consider Jupiter and its four bright Galilean satellites (those moons discovered by Galileo). In binoculars, they look like tiny pinpoints slowly changing places about the planet from night to night. One of these is Io, which has a dozen active volcanoes spewing sulfur all over its surface. Another is Europa, which has an ice-covered *liquid-water ocean* in which scientists think there may be aquatic life-forms. Jupiter's other two big moons, Ganymede and Callisto, are also suspected of having subsurface oceans. Knowing this transforms them into something much more exciting than mere moving points of light!

Perhaps now you better understand why, as previously mentioned, the more you know about the object you're viewing, the more fascinating and meaningful it becomes to you. To fully appreciate and enjoy the wonders described in the various chapters in Part III and Part IV, it's essential to not only see them using your physical eyesight, but with your "mind's eye" as well.

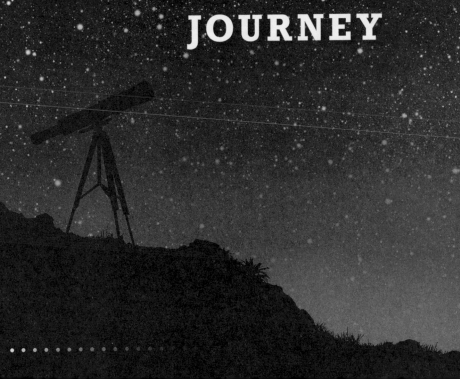

PART II

PREPARING FOR YOUR COSMIC JOURNEY

CHAPTER 4

PASSPORT TO THE STARS

We will now consider the fascinating practical aspects of stargazing in both this and the next chapter. And let's begin with an important definition.

The "official" title of casual stargazing is *amateur astronomy* (as opposed to serious professional astronomy). And a very appropriate term it is, for the word *amateur* is derived from *amator,* which is Latin for "lover." An amateur astronomer is one who loves the stars! It's also worth mentioning that most of today's professional astronomers began as amateurs. And in the early days of astronomy there was no distinction between the two. Many major discoveries were made by "amateurs," including that of the planet Uranus, by William Herschel in England in 1781. And despite the fact that astronomy today is big science, many discoveries have been (and continue to be) made by nonprofessional astronomers using small telescopes, binoculars, and even the unaided eye itself.

While such opportunities to contribute to science remain open to the experienced amateur desiring to do so, this aspect of the hobby won't be covered here, since this book is strictly a sightseer's travel guide to the wonders of the universe.

Let's Get Started

Becoming a stargazer is one of the easiest and least expensive avocations to undertake. In fact, if you go out on a clear night and look up at the sky, you're already a stargazer! But here are a few easy steps to take this a bit further:

EXERCISE:
Basic Stargazing

- Check both the weather forecast for a given evening and the appearance of the afternoon sky (haze, clouds forming, or cloudless blue, as the case may be), anticipating a clear night for stargazing in the offing!

- Dressing appropriately for the season, go outside shortly after sunset and survey the sky for the presence of the Moon and/or bright planets.

- As the sky darkens and night unfolds, look for the brighter stars to begin appearing (the "flowers in the meadows of heaven," as many stargazers regard them)—followed by the starry outlines of various constellations themselves.

- Silently absorb the sublime beauty of the pageantry overhead without attempting to identify what you're seeing, simply *sensing the sacredness* of the sky and expressing gratitude for the privilege of witnessing its majesty!

Beyond this simple act, there are some basic resources that will let you greatly expand upon and enrich your experiences as a stargazer. The world's two leading popular astronomy magazines are *Astronomy* and *Sky & Telescope*. In addition to the fascinating and informative articles, star and planet maps, reports of latest discoveries, and upcoming regional and national astronomy meetings covered in the monthly print editions, the magazines' websites (**www.astronomy.com** and **www.skyandtelescope.com**) contain a veritable treasure trove of information on every aspect of stargazing you will ever need! This includes listings of all the astronomy clubs, planetariums, and observatories open to the public in any area of the U.S.

Attending a club meeting, seeing a planetarium sky show, or going to an observatory open-house night is an ideal way of expanding your hobby beyond that of solitary sky viewing. Indeed, the free public "star parties" sponsored by most astronomy groups are not only a great opportunity to meet fellow stargazers, but also to see and actually look through a variety of both commercial and homemade telescopes.

Learning to See

Strange as it may sound, as a stargazer you have to learn to see—really *see* what it is you're looking at in the sky. There are a number of basic techniques for increasing your ability to view celestial wonders.

— One of the most important of these techniques is **dark adaptation.** We all know that when we turn a light off in a room at night, it takes a few minutes to get used to the dark. The same goes for stepping outside at night from a brightly lit house. You have to give your eyes time to adjust to the darkness before seeing your way around—or being able to glimpse the sky's faint lights. Dark adaptation begins immediately upon placing yourself in the dark and continues to increase for at least 30 minutes, after which the improvement in visibility becomes less obvious.

To maintain your dark adaptation, avoid looking at porch or street lights, or headlights of passing cars. And in checking maps of the sky (star charts), use a red-filtered flashlight or penlight (which doesn't affect dark adaptation) rather than normal white light. These are commercially available, or one is easily made by placing red cellophane over the bulb of an existing flashlight—or painting it with red fingernail polish.

— Another useful technique is that of **averted vision**. The edge of the eye is much more sensitive to low-level illumination than is its center (which is color sensitive). In viewing the sky's fainter objects with the unaided eye or through an optical instrument, instead of staring directly at them look off to one side and they will noticeably increase in brightness. Some dim naked-eye sights to try this on are the Beehive Star Cluster, the Orion Nebula, and the Andromeda Galaxy. (All of the objects mentioned here and below are described in Part IV of this guide).

— There's also the matter of **color perception**. At first glance all the stars appear to be white. But upon closer inspection, you will find that the sky is alive with color! One of the most vivid examples of this will be found in the winter constellation of Orion, the Hunter. The star Betelgeuse in his upper left shoulder is a distinct ruddy-orange hue, while Rigel in his right knee is radiant blue-white in color. To perceive the tint of any star, look directly at it, since as I mentioned this is the color-sensitive part of the eye.

As a nameless writer poetically stated in an obscure little sky guide ages ago, "Every tint that blooms in the flowers of summer, flames out in the stars at night." The famed Pittsburgh telescope maker and astronomy popularizer John Alfred Brashear used to pick flowers from his garden to illustrate the contrasting colors of double stars (to be discussed in Chapter 13) when speaking to schools, long before the advent of color slides.

— One final area in which stargazers can improve how they view the sky is **visual acuity.** This is the ability to see (that is, resolve) fine detail in a celestial object like the Moon or one of the planets, or to separate tight groups of stars. Simply put, the more time you spend observing, the more you'll see of an object. To experience this, make a drawing of the Moon as seen with your unaided eye around the time it is full. Repeat this again for several nights in a row, and you will be surprised to find far more detail in your last sketch than in the first one. Because the eye works in combination with the ultimate computer and "image processor"—the brain!—it can indeed be trained to see anew.

Sky Conditions

As we look out into space at night through the ocean of air above us, there are two states of the atmosphere that affect nighttime sky viewing:

Transparency indicates how clear the sky is, and *seeing* is an indication of how turbulent the air overhead is. Generally speaking, on crystal clear nights the air is unsteady due to upper-atmospheric winds blowing it clean. On such nights, the stars twinkle noticeably, producing flickering, fuzzy images in a telescope. Conversely, on poor-transparency nights the air overhead is stagnant, resulting in very little twinkling and sharp telescopic images.

This is all mainly of concern to telescope users. Unless the sky is noticeably hazy, these conditions have minimal effect on naked-eye or binocular viewing.

An additional concern that impacts the visibility of the night sky is a human-made one—*light pollution.* One of the banes of both amateur and professional astronomy today is the proliferation of outdoor lighting from city and street lights, billboards, shopping centers and car dealerships, stadiums, and other sources. This results from improper shielding, which sends light up into the sky instead of onto the ground where it's needed. Not only does this interfere with looking at the stars; it's also an unnecessary waste of energy and money. There's been a national and international effort under way for some time to curb light pollution, mainly by the International Dark-Sky Association (**www.darksky .org**), which is open to anyone interested in preserving the right to having dark nighttime skies.

Many stargazers today living in brightly lit cities or even in the suburbs find it necessary to travel to dark sites to really see the sky at its best. A state or national park is typically an ideal location if you have one near you—and if you can obtain permission to remain there after sunset, when most close for the night. Also, many astronomy clubs have their own private dark-sky sites available to members.

But you can still enjoy the sky wherever you happen to live. The Moon, planets, brighter stars and constellations, and even some of the more prominent deep-space wonders like star clusters can be seen under all but the brightest of skies.

Incidentally, nature offers its own form of "light pollution"—the Moon! Especially around the time of the full Moon, our lovely satellite lights up the entire sky and makes all but the most luminous of celestial objects difficult to see even from a country setting. But again, the brighter planets and stars are still visible, and the Moon itself is fascinating to look at when fully illuminated despite the lack of obvious craters and mountains (as will be explained further in Chapter 8).

Navigating the Sky

Becoming familiar with the overall appearance of the night sky is best accomplished with the unaided eye rather than through the use of binoculars or telescopes (both of which are discussed in the next chapter). Unlike the relatively limited fields of view of optical instruments, the eye essentially has an "all-sky" view. This makes it easy to identify the various constellations, which serve the same purpose as do states or provinces—to divide up the sky into easily recognizable areas.

Before continuing, I want to share a common complaint of beginning stargazers—that most of the constellations simply don't look anything like the mythological figures the ancients imagined in the sky. I agree completely!

The wonderfully delightful book *The Stars: A New Way to See Them* by H. A. Rey is an absolute must for all star lovers—but especially those just beginning their cosmic journey. Rey has ingeniously redrawn the classic constellation outlines to look like the figures they represent. And they really do! In my opinion, *this is absolutely the easiest and most enjoyable way to identify the constellations* (apps notwithstanding). This book is obviously filling a big need. First published in 1952, it remains in print and still sells briskly today! (Its companion volume, *Find the Constellations,* published two years later, is also still widely used.)

The actual mythology of the constellations in which ancient skywatchers pictured all sorts of heroes and creatures, and their "storybook" of legends and accounts of mighty deeds, is outside the scope of this book. But I'll include the meaning of the names given to the various constellations discussed so you'll have some idea of what they pictured overhead at night. Maybe you can picture them, too!

The monthly star maps contained in the two astronomy magazines mentioned earlier in the chapter are a great place to start identifying the patterns visible in the evening sky. Another valuable and inexpensive resource for this purpose is one of the neat "rotating star charts" (also known as *planispheres*). These can be set to show the sky for any hour of any night throughout the year! One of the best and most affordable is Edmund Scientifics' *Star and Planet Locator,* available at **www .scientificsonline.com**.

It should also be mentioned here that modern technology has given stargazers a great new way to identify stars, planets, and constellations. There is a large array of smartphone and tablet apps available, such as the popular Sky Map (see Appendix A for a more extensive listing), which use GPS reckoning to show you what you are looking at in real time. Simply pointing a tablet, for example, at various parts of the sky will display those constellations (with stick-figure outlines), bright stars, and any planets in a given direction visible from your location at that time and on that date! Most of these devices even identify passages of the brighter satellites and spacecraft, including the International Space Station and the Hubble Space Telescope!

Working with a star map or app, there are two very helpful and simple methods for quickly becoming familiar with the constellations. These involve the use of prominent and easily recognized star groups to point the way to others.

1. One is the **Big Dipper Method.** Most people know that following the two "pointer stars" at the end of the Dipper's bowl northward leads to Polaris, the North or Pole Star, which is part of Ursa Minor, the Little Dipper. But continuing that line northward points to Cassiopeia, the Celestial Queen, on the other side of the pole. And extending the line joining the pointer stars southward points to Leo, the Lion; and its bright star, Regulus. Note also that the Big Dipper's handle is curved: following

the curve downward in the sky brings you to Bootes, the Herdsman; and its bright golden-orange luminary, Arcturus. (This procedure is popularly known as "follow the arc to Arcturus.") Continuing the arc southward brings you to Virgo, the Virgin; and its bright icy-blue star, Spica. Of the 88 official constellations covering the entire sky, 66 are visible from mid-northern latitudes— and it turns out that most of them can be found using the Big Dipper's stars to point the way!

2. The **Orion Method** works in the same manner, and is best used in the winter when the Big Dipper itself lies low above the northern horizon. Looking at a star map, find Orion, the Hunter—the most spectacular of all the constellations visible from mid-northern latitudes! Follow his "belt stars" downward (southeast) in the sky to the brightest star in the entire heavens—Sirius, in the constellation of Canis Major, the Big Dog. Following the belt upward (northwest) brings you to the V-shaped group of stars known as the Hyades in Taurus, the Bull, and its orange luminary, Aldebaran. Continuing that line a bit farther points to the famed Pleiades star cluster (popularly known as the "Seven Sisters"), also located in Taurus.

There is yet another way to identify constellations by making use of what are known as "seasonal geometric shapes." Glancing at a star map during the corresponding four seasons of the year will make it obvious where they are in the sky and how they got their names.

— One of these is the **Summer Triangle** (which is actually visible well into the fall). It consists of the three blue-white diamonds Vega in Lyra, the Lyre; Deneb in

Cygnus, the Swan; and Altair in Aquila, the Eagle. The Triangle is immediately recognizable on a clear night (even from the middle of a city or in bright moonlight), allowing you to instantly identify three constellations and their luminaries!

— The **Fall Square** is actually the Great Square of Pegasus, part of Pegasus, the Winged Horse. A somewhat dim pattern, it's quite a large empty space containing very few visible stars within it. And it's actually more rectangular than square in shape. In fact, if you see it rising in the east, it will even look like a big baseball diamond in the sky! In any case, following a line from the bottom-right-corner star of the Square prolonged diagonally through the upper-left-corner one points to Andromeda, the Princess. Pegasus and Andromeda are actually joined together and share the latter star in common. Following the three additional diagonals across the Square—as well as each side upward and downward in the sky—points the way to several other constellations, as a star map will show.

— Unlike the Fall Square, the **Winter Circlet** (also often referred to as the *Winter Hexagon*) is both dramatic and unmistakable! It consists of a "celestial campfire" made up of eight very bright stars arranged roughly in a circle centered on Orion. Northernmost is golden Capella in Auriga, the Charioteer. Going counterclockwise, we find five bluish-white stars, beginning with Castor and Pollux in Gemini, the Twins. South of them is Procyon in Canis Minor, the Small Dog. Continuing southward is the brilliant diamond Sirius in Canis Major, then westward and upward to Rigel in Orion. Finally, farther north is orange Aldebaran in Taurus. Completing the campfire imagery, in the middle of this stellar circle is ruddy-orange Betelgeuse in Orion—the glowing ember of the campfire itself! You've now found six of the sky's most prominent constellations and eight of winter's brightest stars in just a matter of minutes. How easy was that?

— The last of the seasonal patterns is the **Spring Diamond**. It makes use of four constellations we've already identified. Highest in the sky is the Big Dipper (which is not itself a constellation but rather part of Ursa Major, the Big Bear). The top of the Diamond is the end star in the Dipper's handle. Again following the curve of the handle we come to Arcturus in Bootes, and continuing the arc southward brings us to Spica in Virgo. Its western side is marked by the star at the tip of Leo's tail, called Denebola. (Some stargazers prefer to go a bit farther west to the bright star Regulus, marking the Lion's heart, as the western corner. But doing so distorts the Diamond's shape.) Had we not already used the Big Dipper to identify these four constellations, the Diamond could be used instead. Each of them will lead to other, mostly smaller constellations. Just east of Bootes is Corona Borealis, the Northern Crown; and further east is Hercules, the Kneeler and "muscleman" of the heavens. Just under Virgo is Corvus, the Crow; and Crater, the Cup. West of Regulus and Leo is Cancer, the Crab. In the center of the Diamond we find the two small dim groups: Canes Venatici, the Hunting Dogs; and Coma Berenices, or Berenice's Hair.

Beyond such basic sky orientation, and looking ahead to the time when you may graduate to using binoculars and/or a telescope, you'll need a more detailed celestial road map than those offered in astronomy magazines or on a rotating star chart. Known as *star atlases,* these guides contain various levels of complexity, showing multitudes of stars and deep-space wonders— those objects discussed in Part IV. One of the very best and most useful of these is the compact *Sky & Telescope's Pocket Sky Atlas,* available from **www.shopatsky.com**.

Practical Considerations

There are a number of subtle but nevertheless important factors that impact the overall success and enjoyment of a stargazing session:

— The first concerns **proper dress.** This is of particular importance in the cold winter months of the year, when subfreezing temperatures are often experienced at night. It's impossible to enjoy the views when you're half frozen to death! Proper protection of the head, hands, and feet are necessary, and several layers of clothing are recommended, as opposed to a single heavy one, for thermal insulation. During the summer months, the opposite problem occurs as observers attempt to stay cool. And in addition to very short nights at this time of year, there's the added annoyance of humidity in some regions and flying insects, so beware.

— **Proper posture** is another consideration. It's quite difficult to keep standing and bending your neck upward to look at the sky for very long. Relaxing on a lawn chair is definitely the best way to conduct naked-eye and binocular viewing! In the case of using a telescope, it's been repeatedly shown that the eye sees much more in a comfortably seated position than when standing, twisting, or bending to look into an eyepiece.

— Finally, **rest** and **diet** both play a role in experiencing a pleasurable observing session. Attempting to stargaze when you're physically exhausted is guaranteed to leave you frustrated rather than uplifted. Even a brief catnap before going out to observe after a hectic day is a real help here. Heavy meals can leave you feeling sluggish and unable to function alertly. It's much better to "refuel" following your stargazing session—especially given that most observers find themselves famished then (particularly on cold nights). Various liquid refreshments such as tea, coffee, or hot chocolate can provide a needed energy boost while observing (and warmth when desired).

As an aside, some stargazers recommend having a few glasses of wine before observing since alcohol dilates the pupils, thereby letting in more light. What they fail to recognize is that while this is true, alcohol interferes with production of the eye's "visual purple"—the chemical involved in increasing its sensitivity to faint illumination.

But I personally do find wine and a good astronomy book to be a great way to relax on cloudy nights! And the older the books, the better. I love the observing classics, which hearken back to a time when writers expressed the wonder they saw in the heavens in exalted prose and talked openly about the cosmic Author of the scenes before them. (For some of my favorites, please see Appendix A.)

Returning to Reality

In closing this chapter, there's something else I simply must bring to your attention. One of the curious things that often happen to those of us who become stargazers is that family members, friends, and even concerned neighbors label us as "escapists from reality." They see our nightly vigils under the stars as a desire to get away from the Earth and its many problems rather than dealing with them.

Nothing could be further from the truth! As I pointed out in Chapter 2, stargazing has a very practical value—one that could potentially help save our civilization from self-destructing! But here astronomer Robert Burnham beautifully set the record straight about this lopsided and distorted view in *Burnham's Celestial Handbook:* "To turn from this increasingly artificial and strangely alien world is to escape from *unreality.* To return to the timeless world of the mountains, the sea, the forest, and the stars is to return to sanity and truth." Modern civilization, despite its comforts and advances, is characterized by many developments that are frankly quite disquieting to any sane individual. I've always tried to share with as many people as possible the joy and peace stargazing offers in simply pointing the way to what is *really* reality!

Here's just one example of how I go about doing that. Whenever I've moved into a new neighborhood, one of the first things I do is to introduce myself as an astronomer. I tell the neighbors that if they see me prowling around in the yard at night, I'm just stargazing—and I invite them to stop over for a look through my binoculars or telescope when they do see me out and about.

This not only helps share my lifelong passion for the stars with others, but it also hopefully defuses any possibility of my being a suspected "Peeping Tom" or burglar!

(One time, however, the neighbors didn't believe me and apparently thought my telescope was some kind of "death ray" weapon. Whenever they saw me coming out and setting up at sunset, they called their kids inside and locked the door. Sadly, neither they nor their children ever got to see the wonders awaiting them every clear night during the three years I lived next door.)

Yes, sharing your love of the heavens with others is important. But don't expect *everyone* to catch your excitement and enthusiasm for the stars!

I've mentioned binoculars and telescopes several times thus far. Having now covered the basic elements of stargazing in this chapter, we move on to examine these wonderful devices in the next one. But in doing so, I must warn you—*they can truly change your life forever* as they open up a totally unsuspected and amazing universe to you!

CHAPTER 5

SPACESHIPS OF THE MIND

While the emphasis throughout this book is on celestial sights and events observable with the unaided eye and binoculars, it's important to cover telescopes as well. The reason: once you get hooked on the joys of stargazing, you will sooner or later want to get one to expand your explorations! And having some basic information about these optical marvels will come in very handy when you do. If you prefer to skip the portion of this chapter devoted to these instruments until such a time arrives, do at least read the section on binoculars. You'll find them to be a wonderful and indispensable companion under the stars!

A Wonderful Gift to Humanity

It's a matter of opinion if the telescope (and its eventual spinoff, the binocular) was invented or "discovered." The story goes that a Dutch spectacle maker held up two lenses of different curvature and looking through them saw a distant church steeple close-up.

And here I must share an incredible reading found in the Edgar Cayce material. To me as an astronomer, it's the most astounding of the more than 14,000 he left us. In #1900-1 (the first reading for the 1,900th person he gave them for), it clearly states that someone in re-mote antiquity (around the time of Atlantis) was using "the glass which was found" for studying the stars! The telescope as we know it wasn't invented (rediscovered?) until the early 1600s! Even more amazing—according to Cayce, this original glass was not made by the user, but instead was "found"! If so, then who did actually con-struct it, and even how much earlier in time? (We might also wonder just where this artifact is today.)

In any case, telescopes are marvelous devices for bringing the world that surrounds us—and beyond—into larger and sharper focus. Rather than being viewed as just another technical gadget, they are "windows on creation," "time machines," "mind-expanders," and so much more! A telescope becomes your personal "space-ship" that makes it possible to roam the universe in a way that's surely the next best thing to actually being out there in space yourself.

Robert Frost said in his famous poem "The Star-Splitter" that someone in every town "owes it to the town" to keep a telescope. I definitely agree with him! But I would expand upon this by saying that *someone in every home owes it to the home to keep a telescope.* Without one, you (and your family) are really out of touch with the awesome universe we live in! Australian stargazer Graham Loftus put it this way: "What we need is a big telescope in every village and hamlet and some bloke there with that fire in his eyes who can show something of the glory the world sails in."

Binoculars

These popular glasses are essentially two small telescopes mounted side by side so that both eyes can be used at the same time. They come in many different sizes, types, styles, and magnifications, but they all have one thing in common—they can be used for stargazing, as well as for their more traditional purposes.

Just about everyone has access to a pair, whether for sports events, boating, bird-watching, or other forms of nature study. But few ever think of pointing them skyward at night! Given good optical quality, a pair of binoculars can show you the craters and mountains on the Moon, the four bright satellites of Jupiter, all of the planets except Pluto, comets and asteroids, plus countless wonders beyond the solar system, including even many of the brighter galaxies! They are also superb for viewing eclipses of the Moon and big star clusters like the Pleiades, and for scanning the majestic star clouds of our own Milky Way Galaxy.

It's because of their affordability, ease of use, and wide-bright fields of view that beginning stargazers are encouraged to start with binoculars before graduating to a telescope. They are also ideal for following artificial satellites across the sky, along with passes of the International Space Station and the Hubble Space Telescope. Among the most beautiful sights visible through these glasses are the frequent *conjunctions* (or close pairings) of the Moon and one or more of the brighter planets—especially the crescent Moon and dazzling Venus seen in the same field of view in an evening or morning twilight setting.

There's also one other feature of binoculars worth mentioning: using both eyes gives the amazing illusion of "depth perception" in the sky. This is especially so in the case of the Moon, which looks suspended in space—as in truth it really is!

Binoculars are specified by two numbers: (1) magnification; and (2) aperture, or size of their front lenses, in millimeters. So a 10×50 glass magnifies objects 10 times (thus the ×) and has lenses 50 millimeters (or 2 inches) in diameter. This just happens to be one of the best combinations for stargazing, but keep in mind that *any* pair can be used for this purpose.

Larger sizes and/or more powerful ones typically need to be tripod-mounted in order to steady them. One complaint about all traditional binoculars is that it's hard to do so by hand, which you may well have experienced for yourself. Fortunately, technology has come to the rescue with the introduction of "image-stabilized binoculars." Originally intended for use on rocking boats, these pricey glasses are a real pleasure when used to take in the sights anywhere, including the sky itself.

(If you'd like more information on all aspects of the selection, use, and care of binoculars, as well as telescopes, discussed in the next section, I encourage you to see my profusely illustrated volume *A Buyer's and User's Guide to Astronomical Telescopes & Binoculars,* published by Springer and available at **www.springer.com**. It's based on my more than half a century of experience using these wonderful optical devices.)

Before moving on to explore telescopes themselves, a word about "spotting scopes." These actually *are* telescopes—small-aperture, low-power (typically 40mm to 60mm and 15× to 60×, respectively) refractors (see the next section) intended for bird-watching, spotting targets, and hunting. They are usually equipped with a tabletop tripod or in some cases an adapter for mounting on a car window.

Just as in the case of binoculars, few ever think of using them for stargazing. And while limited in their capabilities, they will provide pleasing views of the Moon, major planets (especially Jupiter and its satellites), and the brighter stars. If you happen to own one of these scopes, take a look at the Moon when it's near first quarter (or half-full, the best time to see its mountains and craters . . . more about this later), and I can promise you that you'll be pleasantly surprised and delighted by what you see!

Telescopes for Stargazing

There are three basic types of optical telescopes used for viewing the heavens:

- Best known is the **refractor** or lens-type, which employs a compound objective (system of lenses) having two or more elements to collect light and bring it to a focus. It's what most people think of when they hear the word *telescope*—someone looking through the end of a long white tube at the sky.

- Another form is the **reflector** or mirror-type, which uses a precision concave primary mirror to do the same.

- The third type is a combination of these two. Called a **catadioptric** or compound telescope, it uses both mirrors and lenses.

Volumes have been written about the advantages of one type of telescope over the others. Suffice it to say that if optically sound, each of them performs equally well and can provide a lifetime of viewing pleasure. The final choice often boils down to a matter of affordability. In any case, purchasing a telescope is a good investment, as unlike other technical devices, they typically *appreciate* in value over time rather than depreciate!

The range of telescope sizes in use by stargazers today is astounding—from handheld or tabletop-mounted little scopes to large observatory-class instruments. Often seen at star parties are the popular "Dobsonian" reflectors, some of which are so huge that they're moved around in trucks and require tall stepladders to reach their eyepieces! Named for their simplified mountings invented by famed telescope maker John Dobson, they are ultra-easy to use and in the smaller sizes are very affordable.

There's also a wide variety of more complex (as well as heavier and costlier) mountings, including computer-controlled ones able to locate thousands of targets automatically from a keypad. However, most of these so-called go-to systems are not quite all they are cracked up to be in terms of setup and actual use under the stars at night. And to us purists, they take much of the fun out of leisurely stargazing using a good star map or atlas to "star-hop" our way to celestial treasures (and seeing unexpected wonders along the way to finding our targets).

Perhaps the most talked-about aspect of telescopes in the popular mind is that of "power." But there are actually *three* types of power!

— Least important of these but uppermost in most people's minds is **magnifying power,** or how much bigger a telescope makes objects than what the eye sees. And here the mistake is often made of judging (and purchasing) a telescope solely on the basis of that power alone. Most small telescopes (especially imported ones) are grossly overpowered.

A useful rule of thumb here is that a magnification of 10× per inch gives the sharpest images and widest field of view. That's 30× for a 3-inch glass and 60× for a 6-inch. (And let me just say here that you can see virtually everything you could possibly want to in the heavens with just 30 power!) A maximum useful magnification of 50× per inch for close-up views of the Moon, planets, and close double stars can be used under good (steady) sky conditions. That's 150× on a 3-inch and 300× on a 6-inch. Anything beyond that is known as "empty magnification"—it makes the image bigger but shows no additional detail and, in fact, often displays it much less sharply than lower powers do. Also, as magnification increases, the field of view (or how much of the sky you see) decreases in direct proportion.

— The most important parameter of a telescope is its **light-gathering power,** which is directly related to its size or aperture. Simply put, the larger the telescope, the more light it collects—so the brighter objects look and the farther out into space you can see. That's why astronomers continue to build bigger and bigger telescopes. (As I write this, both a *1,000-* and a *1,600-inch telescope* are on the planning boards, making them five times and eight times, respectively, the size of the 200-inch Hale reflector on Palomar Mountain!) The surprising thing here is that when you double the aperture of a telescope, you *quadruple* the amount of light it picks up! That's because the area of a circle goes up as the square of the diameter, so there's four times as much light-collecting space on a 6-inch glass as on a 3-inch one.

— Finally, there's **resolving power,** or the ability to show fine features in a celestial object. And here, when you double the size of the telescope, you double the amount of detail that can potentially be seen.

Another rule of thumb concerning telescopes is that *the smaller (and more portable) the scope, the more often it's likely to be used.* Lugging a 50- to 100-pound telescope outside and setting it up in the dark is enough to dissuade many would-be observers, especially on frigid winter nights. I've had the privilege of using some of the largest telescopes in the world, but my personal instruments are a 90-millimeter refractor, a 4-inch reflector, and a 5-inch catadioptric. I can easily pick up any of them in one hand! And yes—I also use 10×50mm binoculars and a 75mm spotting scope for stargazing!

As for commercial sources for telescopes, the two monthly magazines *Sky & Telescope* and *Astronomy* are the best places to look. (See also Appendix A.) The companies that advertise there offer everything from quality beginners' scopes for between $100 and $200 to advanced models costing thousands of dollars. My book on selecting telescopes and binoculars is another resource, listing hundreds of telescope firms covering every price range and level of sophistication imaginable (and showing pictures of many of the instruments).

Another alternative is to make your own telescope. When I built my first telescope at the age of 16 (including grinding and polishing its primary mirror), it was a 6-inch reflector. A scope this size way back then was much too expensive for most stargazers, so they made their own. Mine cost $26 to build—commercially I would have had to spend $300 for the same size instrument.

But today things have changed dramatically with mass production and many more telescope companies in the marketplace. In most cases it's actually less costly to buy a complete instrument (especially reflecting telescopes) than to attempt to make one from scratch. Another option is to purchase the optical components and build a telescope around it (particularly the Dobsonian-style reflector).

Finally, there's the used-telescope market, which often turns up some real bargains. But there's also a lot of risk involved in going this route, since an instrument may look nice but have poor optics, or been subjected to neglect. If it's someone from a local astronomy club selling a scope to upgrade to a larger or different one, you're probably safe in buying it. But it's still best to check it out first. (Again, see my *Buyer's and User's Guide* book for information about testing a telescope's optical quality.)

We've now laid the necessary groundwork for using binoculars and telescopes as your personal "spaceships" for the cosmic journey about to unfold. I would like to end this chapter with a quote from William Tyler Olcott, author of several classic books on stargazing and a mentor of amateur astronomers of the past century: "Lastly, remember that the telescope is a scientific instrument. Take good care of it and it will never cease to offer you many hours of keen enjoyment, and a source of pleasure in the contemplation of the beauties of the firmament that will enrich and ennoble your life." (Incidentally, Olcott's personal telescope was a basic 3-inch refractor.)

And so now . . . let the journey begin!

PART III

WONDERS OF THE SOLAR SYSTEM

CHAPTER 6

OUR DAYTIME STAR

A Glorious Light

We begin our journey by exploring the brightest object in the entire heavens. It's the star we call home—our Sun! (And since in my experience many people still don't realize this, let me state right here and now that *the Sun is a star, and the other stars are suns.*)

And what a wondrous object it is. Measuring some 864,000 miles in diameter, it's big enough to fit more than a million Earths inside of it! Yet, as large as our Sun is, it's actually small compared to the giant and supergiant stars—some of which are big enough to put our *entire solar system* inside of them! It's also our "life-star," supplying virtually all the energy on this planet (except for nuclear energy): the energy in the food we eat; in the gasoline that propels our cars, ships, and planes; and in the coal, natural gas, and fuel oil that heat our homes. All these originally came from the Sun. And to supply us with that energy and to keep us alive, this colossal thermonuclear reactor is converting *five million tons of its mass into energy every second!* Moreover, it's been doing this for the past 4.6 billion years, yet is only midway through its evolutionary life span. This is what it means to be a "star."

And here's another amazing fact. It takes the photons (units of light and heat)—moving at the speed of light—something like a *million years* to get from the center of the Sun to its visible "surface" due to "backscattering" and the opacity of this huge sphere! But once they reach there, it takes only eight minutes for them to travel the 93 million miles to Earth. (For those not familiar with the term *backscattering,* it refers to the fact that photons are continually deflected from their paths directly out of the Sun by running into atoms and bouncing back and forth—like some kind of atomic billiard game.)

Viewing Precautions

Our Sun is a fascinating object and the only star we can see up close. Two of its best-known features are its sunspots and eclipses. But a word of caution is in order: *you must exercise extreme care in viewing the Sun!*

Looking at it through even the darkest pair of sunglasses will not protect you. They may filter out most of its visible light, but harmful ultraviolet and infrared rays will still get through. One traditional recommendation is viewing it through a #14 welder's filter. More convenient are an inexpensive and safe pair of Eclipse Shades, similar to (only in construction!) the 3-D glasses being used in theaters, or a handheld Eclipse Viewer—both of which are available from Rainbow Symphony (**www.rainbow symphony.com/soleclipse**), among other sources.

For up-close views, binoculars are recommended. However, proper filters are an absolute must to avoid serious eye damage or blindness! And the filters must be of the type that *fit over the front of both binocular lenses—not over their eyepieces.* (This is especially true in the case of a telescope and its finder. Many inexpensive small scopes have an eyepiece filter marked "Sun" on it. These are extremely dangerous and often crack due to the intense heat being focused by the telescope itself. Stopping most of the light and heat of the Sun *before* it enters an instrument is the only safe and sane way to view it directly.) One excellent source for optical solar filters is Thousand Oaks Optical (visit **www.thousandoaksoptical.com** and click on the "solar filters" icon).

Another safe but not as effective way to view the Sun is to project its image through a pinhole in a piece of cardboard and onto a white sheet of paper. While the image will be small (depending on the separation of the pinhole and paper), it will reveal the Sun's disk.

Here, I must share a true story that emphasizes the importance of safety when dealing with the Sun. And it's without question the most embarrassing moment in all my many years of lecturing and teaching!

I was conducting a daytime tour for a school group at the Allegheny Observatory in Pittsburgh while I served there as staff astronomer. It was perfectly clear that day, so I was showing the Sun to the group using one of the observatory's large telescopes. Part of this involved a demonstration of just how dangerous our Daytime Star can be in a telescope without proper precautions, during which I was perched at the top of the special ladder used for reaching the eyepiece.

I first showed how a hole could be burned through a telephone book by pointing the instrument at the Sun without a filter. Next, I placed a pencil into the intense beam of sunlight coming out of the eyepiece and it burst into flames.

While I was doing my dog-and-pony show, a boy about ten years old was at the bottom of the ladder and kept saying "Mr. Mullaney . . . Mr. Mullaney!" Now I like kids—but this one was ruining my spiel!

Finally, I looked down at him and asked, "WHAT?"

Then came those words I'll never forget: "Your jacket is on fire!"

The shoulder of my blazer was indeed smoldering! You see, I'd forgotten to cap the telescope's finder (which was a pretty large scope in its own right), and it was burning a hole into the material.

I wasn't quick enough to say that this was all a planned part of the safety demonstration. (Just as well, as other groups from the same school were scheduled to come later that week and would have expected to see my jacket ablaze!)

So, keeping the vital importance of viewing precautions in mind, let's now explore some of the Sun's fascinating features.

Sunspots

The magnetic storms that appear on our star's visible gaseous surface are known as *sunspots*. These range in size from tiny black dots requiring binoculars or telescopes to be glimpsed all the way up to sunspot groups big enough to be seen with the unaided (but properly filtered!) eye. They come and go in an approximately 11-year cycle. Few, if any, of them are to be found at sunspot minimum, when this cycle "bottoms out," while the solar surface may be covered with them around maximum activity, at its peak.

The Sun has revved up for a maximum in 2013. Sunspots are plentiful now and will continue to be so for several years. If you do see some, watch them over a period of days and you will find them moving across the Sun as it slowly rotates. Realize that you are watching a star spin from across a distance of 93 million miles! With binoculars, you may notice that sunspots have a dark inner core, called the *umbra;* and a lighter outer halo, called the *penumbra.*

Now here's an interesting aside concerning sunspots: The famed psychic Edgar Cayce claimed that they are "a natural consequence of the turmoil which the sons of God in the Earth reflect upon same." This echoes the concern of many today that increasing human discord on our planet—combined with thoughtless disregard for the environment—is adversely impacting the Earth's weather patterns, oceans, geological faults, and other vital natural processes. Sadly, this reflects a widespread lack of respect on all levels for our beautiful planet, which is our only home in this vast universe for now (and for the foreseeable future).

The idea here is that the Earth itself is a living organism (the *Gaia hypothesis*), and so too are other celestial bodies—including the Sun. Are human hatred and violence somehow (telepathically?) being transferred to them? If so, this has profound ramifications indeed!

Solar Eclipses

Nature's grandest spectacle is, without question, a *total eclipse of the Sun!* This occurs when the Moon passes directly in front of our Daytime Star. Unlike a total eclipse of the Moon (see Chapter 8), where more than half the world can view the event due to the huge shadow the Earth casts on our satellite, the Sun's shadow is very narrow and averages only a hundred miles or so wide where it touches the surface of our planet. And while several solar eclipses typically happen every year, the shadow cone sweeps out a very narrow path, making it a rare event as seen from any given location. This is why stargazers ("sungazers," in this case!) often travel halfway around the world just to see one—and why costly eclipse cruises are so popular today.

Now here's a truly amazing fact: The Sun is about 400 times the diameter of the Moon. But at its average distance, the Moon is exactly 400 times closer to us, making it possible to perfectly block out the Sun! Many I know believe that the Moon was "parked in orbit" at just the right distance from us by our Creator or some higher intelligence. Considering the profound impact that solar eclipses have had over the centuries on the evolution of human consciousness, this may well prove to be true! This impact has ranged from the ending of local wars in progress, to the worshipping of the "Sun God" by indigenous cultures around the world, to instantaneous enlightenment and cosmic expansion for untold numbers who have witnessed this awesome spectacle. (I've met many of these people and can attest to how utterly life changing a few minutes immersed in the shadow of the Moon with the Sun hidden has been for them!)

A total solar eclipse is of very fleeting duration due to the rapidly moving Moon's shadow—lasting a maximum of about seven minutes and often much less. But in that brief interval, day turns to night, the stars come out, the temperature typically drops 20 degrees or more, and birds return to their nests.

And that's not all. The Sun's glorious pearly outer halo, called the *corona,* hidden in the daytime, comes into full view, and scarlet "flames" can be seen all around the edge of the darkened Sun. Just seconds before and after totality, sunlight passing through valleys on the Moon's surface creates the spectacular "diamond ring" effect. Most significant of all—those viewing this awesome spectacle often let out shouts of joy, tearful cries of ecstasy, and/or fall to their knees and openly praise the Creator of the universe.

I've personally witnessed just one total solar eclipse to date (on March 7, 1970, in Virginia Beach, Virginia, for all of three minutes), but I will *never,* ever forget it!

There are actually two other types of solar eclipses besides a total one. The Moon's orbit is elliptical rather than circular, which means that sometimes it's farther from us than its average distance of 239,000 miles. If an eclipse happens then, its disk is a bit too small to completely cover the Sun. This results in what's known as an *annular eclipse,* where a ring of light from the Sun is still visible around the edge of the Moon. In other cases, the Moon doesn't pass directly across the Sun's center, resulting in a *partial solar eclipse.* Neither of these events is anywhere near as spectacular as a total one, but still definitely well worth watching.

An important note here: During the brief moments of totality, you can safely remove your sunshades or binocular filters to get the full impact of the eclipse. But you absolutely must return the filters _before_ totality ends—which means knowing the exact time of the event for your geographic location. These are published in the astronomy magazines, as well as being listed online. And this holds true only for a total eclipse: for annular and partial ones, filters must be used at all times since part of the Sun remains continuously visible.

Now here's a true story involving a solar eclipse that you may find hard to believe (I still do!). It occurred while I was working at Pittsburgh's Buhl Planetarium and involved the 1970 eclipse I mentioned. We had put out a lot of media publicity about the eclipse (even though this particular one would only be partial as seen there), telling folks what to look for and when. All of the releases, including radio and TV spots, emphasized proper viewing precautions due to the dangers of looking directly at the eclipse with the eyes unprotected.

Well, a person called early one morning a few days before the eclipse and angrily asked: "If this event is so dangerous, then _why_ are you holding it?"

As if we actually "arranged" the eclipse! This clearly shows how far astronomy educators have yet to go in making the public aware of even the most basics facts about the sky.

Other Things to See

When the Sun is seen near the horizon, either rising or setting, it often not only looks huge but also elliptical or egg-shaped. The cause of the former is somewhat of a mystery (see "The Moon Illusion" section in Chapter 8), while the latter is a result of atmospheric refraction (or bending of the Sun's image) by the dense air mass near the horizon. This can sometimes cause the Sun to look double or even as if pieces of it are seemingly lifting off the top!

You'll notice using binoculars that the edge of the Sun when higher in the sky doesn't appear as bright as its center. Known as *limb darkening,* this results from looking through more of its outer atmosphere at its edge. This in turn causes our Daytime Star to appear like a huge three-dimensional globe—which, in fact, it actually is! And there are also transits of objects crossing over the face of the Sun, ranging from the inner planets Mercury and Venus (see Chapter 9) to planes, flocks of geese, and even satellites, including the International Space Station!

It's interesting to note that throughout history there have been reports of unidentified dark objects seen crossing the solar disk, none of which involved any of the foregoing. It was even once thought that there was a planet inside the orbit of Mercury, and it was given the name Vulcan (not the home planet of *Star Trek*'s Mr. Spock!). But we now know that it doesn't exist.

Given a telescope, there are still more fascinating features to see both on the Sun and, using very special filters, *inside* of it as well. Many entire books have been devoted to the pleasures of solar observing for amateur astronomers. And with good reason: again, it's the only star in the entire cosmos that we can see up close and personal.

In the following chapters, we'll examine the fascinating members of the Sun's diverse family, beginning right here at home.

CHAPTER 7

SPACESHIP EARTH

We're All Astronauts!

As you are reading this, the home planet we call Earth is hurtling through space at many different relative speeds and in many different apparent directions. This is what led famed inventor and futurist Buckminster Fuller to call it "Spaceship Earth."

Everyone knows that the Earth rotates on its axis from west to east, causing the Sun (and stars at night) to rise and set. We're spinning at some 900 miles an hour (depending on your latitude—slower toward the poles and faster near the equator). But that's nothing. We're also orbiting the Sun, zipping along at nearly 66,000 miles per hour and taking a year to make a complete circuit. (This means that every time you celebrate your birthday, you've traveled nearly 600 million miles since your last one!)

But there's still more: The Sun is taking the entire solar system on a journey around our vast Milky Way Galaxy at some 550,000 miles per hour. And here, it requires over 220 million years to complete one revolution, or *galactic year.* In addition, our galaxy is part of the Local Group of galaxies within which it's moving. That group in turn is orbiting at the outer edge of a supercluster of some 10,000 galaxies, which is taking part in the overall expansion of the universe itself.

So we've been in "space" and traveling through it all of our lives—making each one of us an "astronaut"!

Atmospheric Wonders

Our planet is overflowing with amazing wonders of every imaginable kind. But here we'll be focusing on what's of special interest to skywatchers: phenomena relating to its atmosphere and objects in orbit just beyond it.

(The atmosphere itself is truly a wonder. If we were to shrink the Earth to the size of a bowling ball and then blow our breath onto the ball, the thin layer of condensation that forms is far deeper than the blanket of air overhead that keeps us alive and protects us from the cold vacuum of space and incoming radiation. Some have referred to it as "the breath of God.")

— One aspect of the atmosphere already mentioned in the section on celestial mandalas in Chapter 3 is the **scintillation** or twinkling of stars due to turbulence, which is especially prevalent close to the horizon.

— On days and nights when there are very high, thin clouds in the sky, you may see **halos** around both the Sun and Moon. These are caused by refraction of sun- or moonlight by ice crystals in the atmosphere and can be used for weather forecasting. Appearing as either a 22-degree-diameter circle (the most common) or a 46-degree one, they signal an approaching front— usually rain in warmer months or snow in colder ones. If the ice crystals in the clouds are oriented just right, you many see tangential arcs and other curious effects. The halos themselves are often colorless but on occasion may appear like faint rainbows with red on the inside and blue on the outside.

— You may also frequently see beautiful prismatic patches on diametrically opposite sides of the Sun as intensifications of the solar halo itself (and, much less often, of the lunar one as well). Called **sundogs** (or **moondogs**), they are not only fascinating to watch but also serve to indicate that precipitation is on the way (generally within 24 hours).

— To my mind, the most amazing atmospheric wonder of all is the majestic **shadow** of the Earth itself. To see it, find a relatively unobstructed eastern horizon (a beach facing east being ideal). On a clear afternoon just as the Sun is about to set in the west, look to the east. There you'll see a bluish-gray, somber-looking area above the horizon that many mistake for darkening storm clouds. Above and in contact with it is a rosy or purplish curved band. And above that is the blue sky itself. That curved arc and its enclosed dull area is the shadow of the Earth projected out through the atmosphere! As the Sun sets and continues to drop below the horizon, the shadow climbs up the eastern sky in response—finally blending into the night sky as darkness falls. In the morning before dawn, the shadow appears in the west and drops lower in the sky as the Sun begins to rise.

And just a word here about sunsets (and sunrises) themselves: The atmosphere acts like an enormous prism, separating the Sun's light into a glorious spectrum of heavenly hues. The variables involved have a seemingly endless number of permutations and combinations. So just as in the case of snowflakes, *no two are ever exactly alike!*

Earth-Orbiting Wonders

Discussing our planet's shadow leads us indirectly to a related realm of other wonders—ones actually above the atmosphere itself in near-Earth orbit. These are artificial satellites and spacecraft. There are many thousands of satellites, ranging from scientific, communication, and weather satellites to GPS and military surveillance ones. The two best-known spacecraft orbiting the Earth are the International Space Station (ISS) and the Hubble Space Telescope (HST). (And the Space Shuttle was formerly included in this list, but it's no longer flying.)

These two, along with hundreds of satellites, are visible to the unaided eye, many often appearing in the sky at the same time as they move from horizon to horizon over a period of minutes. And they range in brightness, with some as visible as Venus and some at the naked-eye limit. Part of this is due to the sheer size of huge objects like the ISS and HST. Others, such as the Iridium communication satellites, have mirrorlike solar panels that brilliantly flash as they rotate and catch the Sun's light. (You can actually get some idea of how fast a satellite is spinning from watching it brighten and fade and brighten again while crossing the sky.)

All of the objects in orbit shine by reflected sunlight, just as do the Moon and planets. And here's the tie-in with the Earth's shadow: After sunset, it climbs ever higher in the eastern sky, being overhead at midnight and then descending in the western sky thereafter. As you're watching a satellite or spacecraft, don't be surprised if it disappears right in front of your eyes! That simply means it's entered the Earth's shadow and is hidden from the light of the Sun.

Times of passage of various satellites over your location can be found online at a number of sites, among them Real Time Satellite Tracking at **www.n2yo.com**, Heavens Above at **www.heavens-above.com**, and **www.J-Pass.com** by NASA. Most fascinating to me are "flyovers" of the ISS, which is the brightest object in orbit. As it silently glides across the sky every 92 minutes at an altitude of nearly 250 miles, it's exhilarating to think that fellow human beings are actually living inside of it and conducting cutting-edge research in space!

Auroras

The *Aurora Borealis* (better known as the "Northern Lights" when seen from the Northern Hemisphere) and the *Aurora Australis* (or "Southern Lights," seen from the Southern Hemisphere) are wonderful atmospheric displays directly tied to sunspot activity. Charged particles from the Sun excite gases like neon and oxygen in our upper atmosphere, causing them to glow. And here we're talking about an amazing light show unlike any earthly counterpart—multicolored undulating curtains, shimmering arcs, and pulsating rays so bright in some cases that they cast shadows on the ground!

While relatively infrequent around sunspot minimum, displays often occur several times a week centered on maximum activity. Whenever a big naked-eye sunspot appears near the center of the Sun's disk during the day, you can be fairly sure of an auroral display that night or the one following. And the higher your latitude (closer to the poles), the more likely that one will be seen. Should a large sunspot or sunspot group be present, there are Internet sites alerting skywatchers to an impending auroral display, such as **www.spaceweather .com**, which shows a real-time image of the Sun daily throughout the year.

A total eclipse of the Sun, as discussed in the last chapter, is without a doubt nature's greatest spectacle. But an intense auroral display is unquestionably its greatest light show! When I witness one, not only do I experience a heady exhilaration but also a very definite spiritual "high." Around the time of sunspot maximum, I make it a practice to always check the sky on clear nights for a possible auroral display—that is, except when the Moon is full and "washes out" the sky. (There have been auroras bright enough to be seen even then, but they are relatively rare.)

UFOs & Nocturnal Lights

There's no question that the *phenomenon* of unidentified flying objects (UFOs) is real—just talk to any astronaut, like Apollo 14's Edgar Mitchell, whom I mentioned in Chapter 3. (Note that this conversation would have to be "off the record," for most of their sightings remain classified. But doing so will leave no doubt in your mind that they saw something extraordinary and are convinced that we are definitely not alone!)

Countless books and papers (many of them scientific) have been written about this subject over the years, and the evidence pointing to the existence of UFOs is persuasive. The real question is: what *are* these mysterious objects? And a related one is: what's their purpose? (And here, on a personal note, I feel that the best movie ever made on the topic is the *original* 1951 version of *The Day the Earth Stood Still*. If you have any interest in this subject at all, you simply *must* watch it!)

While many UFOs have been seen and photographed (and also tracked on radar) in space, the majority of reports concern sightings within our atmosphere. And the most common of these (and the ones you're most likely to experience as a stargazer) are the *nocturnal lights*. These appear as luminous blobs or disks, ranging from single objects to entire formations (typically either in a V-shaped or circular formation). And while they may actually briefly hover over the observer (sometimes at close range), more often they are moving about the sky—all in eerie silence.

Most UFO researchers (and witnesses) agree that there appears to be intelligence behind the phenomenon. There's also general agreement that it has something to do with the expansion of human consciousness, for seeing one leaves most witnesses in awe and open to the existence of other realities besides our own. (This has been the opinion of such noted and respected, academically based authorities over the years as J. Allen

Hynek, Ph.D.; John Mack, M.D.; and Jacques Vallée, Ph.D., among others.)

I'm frequently asked at lectures if I've ever seen any UFOs. Actually I have, on a couple of occasions. The one that really stands out happened on a fall evening in the late '60s over downtown Pittsburgh. And there were many people all across the city who saw it!

The Allegheny Observatory, where I was working at the time, was conducting its annual open-house night (as most such institutions regularly do for the public). In addition to the observatory's own instruments, members of the local astronomy club had dozens of their telescopes set up on the front lawn to help handle the crowd, which was estimated at nearly a thousand.

Around 10 P.M., a glowing, featureless golden disk about the size of the full Moon appeared over the skyscrapers of the city, flipped on its side like a coin, and then became a luminous line hanging in the sky. Within a matter of seconds, it disappeared as the line collapsed inward on itself, just the way an old-fashioned TV picture used to do when the set was shut off. Just as it did, fighter jets from the local Air National Guard came in at a very low level over the city, and circled around and around for several minutes. (Apparently they still had the object on radar even though it had disappeared from view.)

A related "sighting" that was perhaps even more thrilling occurred a decade before, in the same place during the same kind of event, on the evening of October 4, 1957. But it wasn't a UFO. Perhaps that date rings a bell? It was the beginning of the Space Age, with the launching of Sputnik by Russia! At this earlier open house, large numbers of us got to see the first artificial satellite on its initial pass over the United States. How very awesome! Talk about a "night to remember." Just thinking about it still sends chills up my spine more than half a century later.

While this was certainly a one-of-a-kind event, I should point out that one of the perks of stargazing is always the possibility of seeing something strange (and wonderful!) overhead. (I often hear people say that they've never seen anything unusual in the sky. And I simply ask them where they spend most of their time at night. Indoors, and not outside looking up, as we stargazers do!)

Living here on the surface of the Earth, we can only see one part of our beautiful planet at any given time—what's right around us where we are. But in the next chapter we have an opportunity to view an entire amazing world at a single glance. It's none other than our companion in space, the Moon!

CHAPTER 8

QUEEN OF THE NIGHT

The World Next Door

At an average distance of 239,000 miles, our lovely Moon is the only celestial body in the nighttime sky whose surface can be seen without optical aid. And with a diameter a quarter that of the Earth itself, it is unique among all the satellites in the solar system—none of which are anywhere near that relative size compared with the planets they orbit. Indeed, some planetary scientists actually consider the Earth-Moon combo to be a double planet! A *satellite* orbits its parent planet, so technically the Moon *is* one, since it orbits the Earth. But the two bodies are so big in relation to each other that they could be looked upon as two planets. Indeed, the Moon is nearly as large as the planet Mercury!

As the Moon orbits the Earth approximately every month, it goes through the familiar phases from new Moon (when the illuminated portion faces away from us), to crescent, to first quarter (or half-illuminated), to gibbous, and finally to full Moon (at which time its fully illuminated surface presents itself to us). The phases then repeat the same sequence in reverse order.

Many are understandably puzzled why the half-full Moon is called the first quarter: it's simply because our satellite is *one-quarter of the way around its orbit* when seen half-illuminated in the evening sky (and three-quarters of the way seen at last quarter in the morning sky).

Earthshine

One of the most beautiful sights presented by the Moon occurs when it's in the crescent phase—either in the evening sky after sunset or the morning sky before sunrise. Known as *earthshine,* this is when the unilluminated portion of the Moon can be faintly seen lit up. In the evening, this is sunlight reflected mainly from the Pacific Ocean (where the Sun is still shining) onto the Moon's surface, while in the morning it is light reflected from the Atlantic Ocean, where the Sun has already risen.

Easily seen with the unaided eye, earthshine is especially spectacular in binoculars! The Moon's major surface features can actually be glimpsed bathed in this eerie half-light, the intensity of which depends on the amount of cloud cover over the oceans at the time. An astronaut standing on the Moon in this earthshine would find it some 80 times as bright as the full Moon is here on Earth—with the Earth itself appearing four times as large in the sky as the Moon does to us!

Touring an Alien Landscape

Nothing beats embarking on a "sightseeing tour" of the Moon's surface using binoculars (which should ideally be tripod-mounted for best results). And here you'll need a lunar "road map" to find your way around. A number of them are available without cost online (see Appendix A), while Sky Publishing (*Sky & Telescope* magazine) offers a selection of relatively inexpensive ones at **www.shopatsky.com.**

Now here's a fact that comes as a surprise to most beginning stargazers: the best time to view our satellite's surface features is *not* at full Moon, as many believe, but rather around the half phases! This is because the Sun is shining directly onto the Moon when full, and virtually no shadows are cast by its surface features—and it's their shadows that cause them to stand out in sharp relief. Around the quarter phases, the Sun is shining in at a glancing angle (essentially coming in "from the side" of the Moon), and the surface features cast striking relief-exaggerating shadows.

Here are a few of the most obvious features of the Moon to the unaided eye and in binoculars:

— The dark and relatively smooth areas are known as the **maria**, which is Latin for "seas." They were so called by pre-telescopic observers since it was thought they were large expanses of water or oceans, which explains the fanciful names given to them, such as the Sea of Tranquility, the Bay of Rainbows, and the Ocean of Storms. After the invention of the telescope, it became obvious that they are actually plains of solidified lava dating from the Moon's early history.

— Best known of the Moon's features are the **craters**, which range from huge structures more than a hundred miles across down to ones covering less than a mile. Many have central peaks, which often catch the Sun's rays while the craters themselves still lie in darkness, looking like stars or lights on the lunar surface!

— As the *terminator,* or dividing line between day and night on the Moon, slowly advances, new features are continually unveiled, including majestic **mountain ranges**, named for their earthly counterparts, such as the Alps and Apennines, accompanied by deep **valleys** or gorges, like the amazing Alpine Valley.

— And while the full Moon lacks the dramatic surface relief of the other phases, there is one fascinating feature best seen at that time: bright **rays** appear to be "spraying" from many of the craters, most obvious of which are those radiating outward from the crater Tycho and stretching across the lunar surface all the way to the back side!

Here are a few additional facts about our Moon worth mentioning: Due to subtleties in its orbital motion, it turns out that the phases don't repeat exactly for at least seven years—so even familiar features continually look different from month to month. And the back side of the Moon isn't "the dark side," as so many believe! It goes through phases *complementary* to those of the front side. At new Moon, the entire back side is illuminated as it faces the Sun, and the front side is completely dark. Conversely, at full Moon, the back side is completely dark and the front fully illuminated. When the Moon looks half-lit to us at its quarters, the back side is also half-lit. Finally, the full Moon is some *12 times* as bright (not twice, as you might think) as when half-full due to the near-total absence of shadows on its surface at that time.

Talking about the front and back side of the Moon, this will be a good place to answer a question that's often asked about our lovely satellite: If the Moon rotates (which it does!), why do we never see the back side? Good question! That's because it *rotates in the same period as it revolves around the Earth.*

To see this, stand in the middle of a room and have someone face you several feet away. Now, ask your partner to slowly move around you while always facing in the same direction (which means that the person is not rotating on his or her "axis" but only revolving in "orbit" about you). As you follow this movement, you'll first see the side of your partner's face and then the back of his or her head! If the Moon didn't rotate on its axis, we would see its back side every month, just as in this example. (Actually, we do see a small percentage of it as a result of a slight orbital "wobbling" of our satellite, called *libration*.)

Occultations

In its never-ending orbital journey around the sky, the Moon moves roughly its own diameter eastward every hour. As a result, it frequently passes in front of stars and other celestial bodies, including (though much less frequently) one of the planets, in what is known as an *occultation*.

Before full Moon, objects disappear at its dark limb (or edge) and reappear about an hour later at its illuminated one. After full Moon, they disappear at its bright limb and reappear at its dark one. And these events are quite sudden and dramatic, the star blinking out (or on) as if someone turned off (or on) a light switch!

Most dramatic of all is an occultation of a big bright star cluster like the Pleiades. You can actually watch one star after another disappearing from view and later re-appearing again as the Moon silently glides across this stellar clan. While occultations of bright stars, planets, and clusters like the Pleiades *can* be seen with the un-aided eye, binoculars greatly enhance the view (and impact!) of these events.

Note that especially when passing over a star cluster, the Moon looks suspended three-dimensionally in front of it (as it actually is). And in the case of any occultation, *realize that you are watching another world move right before your eyes!* This is just one of many examples that the nightly sky drama unfolding overhead is not a static one—but rather it's alive with exciting, ongoing action performances!

Lunar Eclipses

Most spectacular and fascinating of all the events in-volving our Moon are its eclipses, during which it moves into, through, and then out of the Earth's huge shadow-cone. The shadow itself has a dark inner core, called the *umbra,* and a much lighter outer area surrounding the umbra, known as the *penumbra.* When the Moon passes through the penumbra, its dimming is barely notice-able—but when in the umbra, it's quite dramatic!

A *total lunar eclipse* happens when the Moon passes entirely within the umbra, while a *partial lunar eclipse* occurs with part of our satellite remaining outside of it. And while there have been very dark eclipses during which the Moon has nearly vanished from view, more typically it can still be seen bathed in a beautiful rosy or coppery half-light. This is sunlight bent into the shadow by the Earth's atmosphere acting like a lens. (Incidentally, the well-known phrase *once in a blue moon* has nothing to do with its color but the fact that there happen to be two full Moons within the same month.)

The Moon's visibility during totality depends on such factors here on Earth as the percentage of cloud cover, smoke from forest fires, and ash from volcanoes that may be venting at the time. The dates and times of upcoming lunar eclipses are given in *Astronomy* and *Sky & Telescope* magazines, as well as online and in almanacs.

Eclipses of the Moon can definitely be enjoyed with the unaided eye alone, but given a pair of binoculars, they take on an entirely new level of excitement. In either case, you can actually see our lovely Queen of the Night slowly moving first into and then out of the Earth's shadow. And something important to note here as you do: the shadow on the lunar surface is *curved, not straight.* This is direct visible proof that the Earth itself is round—a fact recognized by many ancient skywatchers despite the persistent belief that the world was flat.

The Moon Illusion

One of the enduring mysteries of astronomy is why the Moon (and the Sun as well) looks so huge when it's rising or setting close to the horizon. Many different theories have been put forth, but none really explain this fascinating phenomenon. One is that near the horizon there are things like houses and trees to compare the Moon's size with, while there are none when it's overhead. In fact, photographs show that the Moon actually appears somewhat *larger* overhead than at the horizon because it's then closer to us by the 4,000-mile radius of the Earth. And what's really strange about this illusion is that when you look at the Moon through some kind of aperture such as a cardboard paper-towel tube, it immediately shrinks to its normal-looking size! (People greatly overestimate the Moon's apparent size in any case, with most saying that a quarter held at arm's length is required to cover it. In fact, a dime more than suffices.)

So it appears that the cause of the illusion is physiological, originating in the eye-brain combination of the observer. But just exactly what that mechanism is remains a mystery. Come up with the answer and you could become famous!

Journeys to the Moon

We're all familiar with the amazing spaceflights to the Moon made by the Apollo astronauts in which 12 men from Planet Earth walked its surface. The most dramatic and accurate account of these epic voyages is the wonderful 12-part docudrama series produced by Tom Hanks entitled *From the Earth to the Moon* (named after the classic Jules Verne novel of the same title). What's of special interest to us here is that a number of the astronauts had "unusual" experiences on their trips, ranging from blobs of light observed pacing their spacecrafts in lunar orbit to spiritual "highs" and other personal revelations on the Moon's surface.

One widely quoted instance is Jim Lovell's cryptic message to NASA after rounding the far side of the Moon for the first time in history, on Christmas Eve of 1968: "Houston, Apollo 8. Please be informed, there is a Santa Claus." The official explanation is that this was simply a Christmas greeting. Others say it was the euphoria of having successfully gone into lunar orbit and not having missed the Moon! But many believe instead that this was actually a coded message for something very unusual the astronauts saw on the back side of the Moon.

And here it should be noted that ever since the invention of the telescope right up to the present day, there have been reports of "activity" seen on the Moon by both amateur and professional astronomers (including the great William Herschel, founder of sidereal astronomy). Known as *transient lunar phenomena* (or TLPs), these include flashing lights, purplish glows (especially ones involving the crater Aristarchus), and temporary obscurations of surface features within large craters such as Plato. In my many years of "moongazing," I've seen a number of these events myself and can personally vouch for their reality!

Consider, also, the possibility that long before Apollo, others may have "traveled" to the Moon! An early example involves the great astronomer Johannes Kepler, whom I've mentioned in previous chapters. He published what is considered a fantasy about a trip to the Moon entitled *Somnium,* which is Latin for "The Dream." In it, a student of the equally famed astronomer Tycho Brahe is transported to the Moon by "occult forces" and, among other things, gives a description of how the Earth looks from there. It's interesting to note that Kepler *was* a student of Tycho's!

Both Carl Sagan and the writer Isaac Asimov considered this to be the very first real work of science fiction. That may well be true, but to me Kepler's "dream" has always sounded like an eyewitness account of an actual journey to the Moon. Perhaps he had an out-of-body experience and astral-traveled there?

This in turn brings me to the psychic Edgar Cayce once again. He gave readings for a person whom he said had actually made two "sojourns" to the Moon in the distant past!

The fact that human beings have gone to the Moon and physically walked on its surface is an utterly amazing technological feat, one certainly unparalleled in all of history. (Sadly, when asked each year what day July 20 is, few people know or remember. I refer to it as "Moon Day" and feel strongly that it should be a national/international holiday so we'll never forget what happened on that date!) It's also a triumph of the human spirit to have realized the age-old dream of finally being able to leave the confines of Earth and travel into space.

I'm certainly a great proponent of space exploration —of channeling our energies into probing that "final frontier" that *Star Trek* always talked about, as an alternative to the ongoing warfare and mindless materialism that characterizes our civilization today. Those who say that money spent on the space program is a waste simply don't know what they're talking about! The ROI (return on investment) of the entire space program since its inception right up to the latest spacecraft exploring the planets and orbiting telescopes surveying the universe itself is estimated to be *700 percent!* That's just in terms of new technology, new industries, and new jobs. It doesn't include the intangible (and priceless) benefits of elevating the human condition on this planet above the mundane and the basic struggle for survival.

But advances also often take us back a step in some ways as well. Now that we have gone to the Moon, and with plans to return and colonize it, much of its romance and magic and mystery have vanished. Its parched, desolate, airless surface, having temperature extremes ranging from above the boiling point of water in direct sunlight to nearly 250° F below zero in the shadows, is not the issue. Those facts were known long before we ever went there. It's realizing that the beautiful, ethereal, unreachable, smiling Queen of Night has now become another world to be conquered.

Meditating on Moonbeams

I'd like to conclude our survey of the lovely Queen of the Night by mentioning its role in meditation. In Chapter 3 I discussed using the stars as celestial mandalas for this purpose. Much less obvious and riveting than the spectacle of a sparkling, colorful bright star is the magical soft radiance of the Moon. Especially around the time that it's near its full phase, the Earth's satellite bathes the landscape in a subtle bluish light (the color actually results from the same cause as the sky being blue in the daytime—that is, from the scattering of sunlight).

And it's indeed a soothing, peaceful light. The great Hindu sage Paramahansa Yogananda in his wonderful little book *Metaphysical Meditations* devotes a section to meditating on moonbeams, calling them a "mystic light." He says to meditate "in the cool moonbeams of your calmness" until you "behold the Universe as Light." This enlightened being was very much in tune with the cosmos, and he considered every "star blossom of heaven" to be a window through which to behold God! (For those who love to meditate, this pocket-size treasure trove is available from the Self-Realization Fellowship at **www.yogananda-srf.org.**)

Having now explored our own planet and its satellite, we move on to survey the other members of the Sun's fascinating family in the next two chapters.

CHAPTER 9

THE WANDERERS & THEIR SATELLITES

The Moving "Stars"

There were five of them, all known since remote antiquity. They were bright and readily visible to the unaided eye. And unlike the fixed stars, which never moved in relation to each other, these objects slowly drifted around the sky along a pathway called the *ecliptic*. They eventually came to be called *planets*, which is Greek for "wanderers," and named after various gods. In order of distance from the Sun they are: Mercury, Venus, Mars, Jupiter, and Saturn.

Not only do they move, but something else sets them apart from stars—they don't twinkle, but instead shine with a steady light. (The reason for this is a bit subtle: Stars are so distant that they essentially shine by a single incoming ray of light, which is easily affected by atmospheric turbulence. Planets, on the other hand, are relatively nearby and have sizable disks, which send out bundles of rays that are largely unaffected by turbulence.) The remaining planets, Uranus, Neptune, and Pluto (which has been demoted to a "minor" one—more about this later!), were all discovered in relatively recent times using telescopes.

We shall now explore each of these restless worlds, no two of which are alike. And here it should be mentioned that none of them are at all hospitable to human beings without life support and extreme protection of the physical body. Yet, just as in the case of the Moon, there are those who claim to have visited these planets in their "astral bodies."

Mercury

This swift "Winged Messenger of the Gods" of mythology is well named, for Mercury is the most rapidly moving of all the planets. It's also closest to the Sun, never straying far from it in the sky. It comes into view after sunset in the evening—or before sunrise in the morning—for a week or two at a time, and then quickly disappears into the Sun's glare. So fleeting is it that it's often been said that a number of famous astronomers of the past, including Copernicus, never saw it. But at least in the case of the "Father of the Copernican Revolution," this appears to be only a myth.

These stories have, sadly, discouraged many stargazers I know from ever trying to find Mercury. But it *is* clearly visible to the unaided eye if you know when and where to look for it. Suffice it to say, there is great satisfaction in seeing this elusive object, especially for the very first time! As with all of the planets, consult *Astronomy* or *Sky & Telescope* magazine (online or the monthly print versions) for its current visibility.

Incidentally, since Mercury orbits the Sun inward of us, it goes through phases like those of the Moon. But being only about 2,900 miles in diameter, its apparent disk is very small, and a telescope is required to see the phases. Also, as is generally well known, this planet has virtually no atmosphere—and due to its proximity to the Sun (its average distance being 36 million miles), it's actually hot enough on its surface to melt lead! (The legendary planet Vulcan that supposedly existed even closer in than Mercury was discussed in the chapter on the Sun.)

Venus

As the third-brightest object in all the heavens, after the Sun and the Moon, this radiant "Goddess of Love and Beauty" of mythology is truly a magnificent sight to behold! When seen in the sky after sunset, it's popularly called the *Evening Star* and in the morning before dawn the *Morning Star* (it *is*, of course, a planet—not a star).

It's also sometimes referred to as the Earth's "Sister Planet" since both worlds are nearly identical in size. But that's where the resemblance ends. Venus has an atmosphere some *90 times* denser than that of Earth, which traps the Sun's heat into a bizarre "runaway greenhouse effect." This in turn results in a planet-wide surface temperature close to 900° F—twice that of an oven, and much hotter than Mercury despite being nearly twice as far from the Sun!

It's this heavy cloud cover that makes Venus appear so bright in our skies, reflecting much of the visible light it receives from the Sun. At its *elongations* east of the Sun in the evening and west of it in the morning, it's visible for many hours. It continues to increase in brightness as it both closes in on our side of the Sun and at the same time comes nearer to us. As in the case of Mercury, Venus goes through phases.

Now here's a truly surprising fact: Unlike our Moon, Venus (and Mercury) is actually brightest when in the crescent phase rather than when fully illuminated! That's because when full, it's on the far side of its orbit beyond the Sun and fairly small in apparent size, but when in the crescent phase it's much closer to us. As a result, its big crescent is many times larger in apparent size than the disk of the full Venus—so much so that it can be seen in binoculars!

Also, when at its most radiant (about a month before it moves from the evening sky into the morning one and a month after being there), the planet can actually cast shadows on a snow-covered landscape! Spreading a white sheet on the ground behind you in the absence of light pollution or moonlight will also show your shadow. (Again, this is possible because Venus reflects more than 75 percent of the light it receives from the Sun.) In addition to being the brightest of all the planets, it also approaches the closest to us, at a minimum distance of some 26 million miles (much nearer than Mars comes).

Since Venus is so brilliant, this is an appropriate place to talk about *conjunctions*—or the close pairing of two or more celestial objects in the sky. I've already mentioned these in connection with the Moon and one of the brighter planets while discussing ideal targets for binocular observing in Chapter 5. But two or more planets can also occupy the same part of the sky, or a planet and a bright star or cluster of stars. When Venus is involved, the scene itself is guaranteed to be spectacular!

But there's more. The night-to-night orbital motion of one planet with respect to another—or of a planet in reference to a star—is especially noticeable during a conjunction. This offers a firsthand opportunity to see why ancient stargazers called these restless worlds "wanderers"!

Mars

This planet is the infamous "God of War," so named because of its distinctive ruddy-orange hue. But its color has nothing at all to do with war and bloodshed. Mars is an *oxidized* world—in other words, it's rusty! And what's exciting about this is that by heating its desert sands, it would be possible to liberate oxygen and water vapor, both of which are essential for life. Those space scientists now actively involved in planning the eventual colonization of the Red Planet (as it's popularly known) are, in fact, counting on doing just that.

But Mars has long been associated with life elsewhere, both in fiction and in fact. This can be traced largely to the sensational announcements by the Italian astronomer Giovanni Schiaparelli in 1877 and later by Percival Lowell in America that the Martian surface is covered by a network of channels or "canals." Lowell in particular claimed that these served the purpose of bringing water from the melting polar caps to this largely dry desert world. Sadly, this romantic idea was eventually proved to be false by various spacecraft that both orbited Mars and landed there. The canals themselves were shown to be an illusion caused by the tendency of the human eye to connect spots together into lines. And yet, having viewed the planet for many years with large backyard and observatory telescopes, and seen them for myself, I can tell you that they certainly do look real!

So deeply rooted was the idea of life on Mars that it led to the publication in 1897 of the classic novel *The War of the Worlds* by H. G. Wells in England—followed years later in 1938 by the notorious radio broadcast adaptation by Orson Welles that set off a national panic in the U.S. People tuning in to this CBS broadcast actually believed that Martians had landed in New Jersey and were on their way to New York City. Many alarmed listeners fled their homes, missing the disclaimer that it was only a fictional play. I've listened to the original *Mercury Theatre* broadcast on tape and can readily understand how this got out of hand! (The coincidence of the names of the author and narrator is indeed fascinating, to say the least!)

There's also the famous "Face on Mars" and other unusual-looking structures found in photographs of the planet taken by one of the Viking orbiters. Like the canals, these too have been attributed to illusions—in this case tricks of light and shadow (although not everyone is convinced of this).

The question of microbial life on Mars is still being debated, both in data from the Viking landers and also in analyses of a piece of the planet that bounced off and eventually landed here as a meteorite. It's hoped as I write this that the latest and most advanced probe to land on the planet, named Curiosity, will finally be able to settle this question.

Perhaps, in the final analysis, the late Ray Bradbury was right in his prophetic 1950 science-fiction novel *The Martian Chronicles* when he said that in effect *we are the Martians!* He was referring to that time in the future when we've settled on the planet and become its inhabitants. And as mentioned previously, heating the Martian soil will liberate both water vapor and oxygen. Futurists are counting on this to "terraform" the planet for human colonization!

As the most fascinating of all the planets, here are some interesting facts to ponder about Mars as you look up at it on a clear night. With a diameter of about 4,200 miles, it's only about half the size of Earth. Its day is just over half an hour longer than ours, and the tilt of its axis is nearly identical, resulting in seasons like the Earth's. But being farther from the Sun than we are, it takes Mars twice as long to orbit it, and its seasons are therefore twice as long as ours.

About every 26 months, it comes to *opposition* to the Sun—meaning that it's opposite the Sun in the sky, rising in the east as it sets in the west. This is also when Mars is nearest to us, coming to within 34 million miles at its most favorable approaches. (The planet's orbit is elliptical rather than round, so at some oppositions it's closer than at others.)

The Martian atmosphere is extremely thin and composed mainly of nitrogen, while the mean surface temperature ranges from −60° F to above the freezing point of water in the tropics. Water-vapor clouds and occasional planet-wide dust storms are other features. Water itself is present in the polar ice caps mixed with carbon dioxide (or "dry ice"). As the caps alternately melt in the summer months, the dark gray areas change in intensity and turn greenish. But this seasonal variation isn't due to vegetation, as was originally believed, and the exact cause is still not fully understood or agreed upon by planetary scientists.

Despite its proximity and centuries of scrutiny—and all that we appear to know about the planet today—Mars continues to mystify and intrigue us. Here are some examples:

— It has two very tiny moons, named *Phobos* and *Deimos* (which require a fair-sized telescope to be glimpsed). Only some ten miles and five miles in diameter, respectively, they may well be captured asteroids. But the orbit of Phobos itself is so unusual that it led the eminent Russian astrophysicist I. S. Shklovsky to propose in the mid-20th century that it's actually an artificial satellite launched by an advanced but long-dead Martian civilization!

— Even stranger, fully 150 years before the two small moons of Mars were actually discovered in 1877, Jonathan Swift in his novel *Gulliver's Travels* uncannily predicted their presence, even giving their correct orbital periods! How did he know about them? Some say it was just a lucky guess. But I wonder? Could he have perhaps astral-traveled there?

— Also, flashes have been seen on the surface of the planet, and in at least one case a cloud moving outward into space from off its limb. These have been attributed to various causes, including meteor impacts, volcanic activity, and reflections from icy patches.

To think that all we've discussed in this section is contained in that ruddy point of light we call Mars. As I've previously pointed out, foreknowledge about a celestial object, combined with looking at it both in mind and sight, truly adds an exciting new dimension to the night sky above our heads!

Jupiter

Appropriately for the "King of the Gods," this giant world, 86,000 miles in diameter, is the largest of all the planets and big enough to contain some 1,200 Earths! And yet it spins on its axis in less than ten hours—causing it to look noticeably flattened at its poles and its dense clouds to be drawn out into parallel bands as seen in a telescope.

Like all four of the giant outer planets, Jupiter's atmosphere is largely hydrogen, with smaller amounts of helium, methane, and ammonia—all at temperatures hundreds of degrees below zero F. The most famous feature of its atmosphere is the *Great Red Spot* (again, only visible with a telescope but often seen in photographs of Jupiter). This huge cyclonic disturbance measures some 25,000 miles from tip to tip (or the circumference of the Earth itself!) and rotates with the planet. It's been seen since the earliest telescopic observations and is visible throughout Jupiter's 12-year orbit of the Sun. But it does change in both visibility and color—often appearing more of a salmon hue than red.

The most fascinating feature of Jupiter for the stargazer is its amazing retinue of moons, which number 63 and counting! Indeed, it's almost like a miniature solar system. There are four major ones, known as the *Galilean Satellites,* after Galileo, who discovered them with his primitive telescope. Each is a world in its own right, two of them being about the size of Mercury. As already mentioned in Chapter 3, seen in binoculars they look like tiny pinpoints of light hugging the planet and slowly changing positions relative to it from night to night.

One of these is *Io,* which has a dozen active volcanoes spewing molten sulfur all over its surface. Another is *Europa*—which, as I mentioned at the end of Chapter 3, has an ice-covered *liquid-water ocean* in which scientists think there may be aquatic life-forms! Jupiter's other two big moons, *Ganymede* and *Callisto,* are also suspected of having subsurface oceans.

Amazingly, some stargazers blessed with superb vision have reported actually seeing some of these satellites with the unaided eye—and there are even such accounts going far back into antiquity before their nature was known! *Astronomy* and *Sky & Telescope* both show the nightly positions of these four moons whenever Jupiter is visible.

There are some other aspects of the Galilean satellites worth noting. Although a telescope is needed to experience them, it's certainly worth knowing about them (especially if you plan to eventually get one of these "magic glasses" for yourself):

As the moons orbit Jupiter, they often *transit* (or pass) in front of it and cast their inky-black shadows onto the cloud tops below. They also orbit behind the planet in *occultation* disappearances and reappearances. Most spectacular of all, the moons undergo *eclipse* disappearances and reappearances as they move into, and then out of, Jupiter's enormous shadow.

What a thrill as a stargazer to watch one of these moons disappear or reappear promptly on schedule from across the gulf of interplanetary space right in front of your eyes! (Their ingress and egress into and out of the shadow, respectively, takes only a couple of minutes, the outer moons moving more slowly since they are farther from the planet.) The times of these various events are conveniently listed in *Sky & Telescope* during those months when Jupiter is well placed for viewing. Some refer to this dynamic world as a "three-ring circus" because of all its satellite activity—but actually it's a *four*-ring one!

Eclipses of Jupiter's moons were what was used to measure the speed of light for the first time. When astronomers calculated the times of these satellite events based on observations made when the planet was at its minimum distance from us of 365 million miles (at opposition), it was noticed that they occurred later than predicted the farther Jupiter was from us in its orbit. It was soon realized that this was because the light from there required more time to reach us. This meant that it must be moving at an amazing but finite speed (186,000 miles per second!) and not instantaneously, as was the belief at the time.

Reliving these historic observations and calculating the speed of light is something advanced amateur astronomers can do right in their backyards using small telescopes. The exhilaration of determining and verifying one of the most widely known and quoted fundamental constants of nature for yourself must be experienced to be appreciated! (While somewhat involved, this calculation uses the relation *Rate = Distance/Time* as its basis. It's a matter of timing eclipses at varying known distances in Jupiter's orbit and seeing how these times differ from what they would be if light traveled instantaneously.)

Saturn

The slow-moving "God of Time" is generally considered to be the most beautiful and "otherworldly" sight in the entire heavens! This magnificent ringed planet definitely is *the* iconic image of astronomy. And while the pictures of Saturn taken by spacecraft like the Voyager and Cassini missions, as well as the orbiting Hubble Space Telescope, are truly amazing, seeing the planet "live" with your own eyes is far more thrilling!

I'll certainly never forget my first view of Saturn, at the age of 12, through my uncle's small telescope. I was so excited that I ran up and down the streets in our neighborhood pounding on everyone's door to come out and see this awesome wonder of the sky! Viewing it in later years through large observatory telescopes, I can only say that Saturn has to be seen to be believed in such instruments. Words utterly fail to convey its ethereal beauty. Even if you don't own a telescope yourself, you simply *must* attend an observatory open-house night or astronomy-club "star party" when Saturn is visible and experience its wonder for yourself. Prepare to be awed!

As indicated, viewing the rings of Saturn requires a telescope—one magnifying at least 25 times (25×) or so. With the exception of high-power glasses that magnify that much, binoculars will only show Saturn as egg-shaped. But that means at least you are seeing the *presence* of the rings, which is exciting in itself. This is basically what Galileo saw when he first looked at the planet with his primitive telescope. However, he actually reported seeing *three objects* in contact with each other (the ball of the planet itself and the unresolved rings on either side of it).

It was the Dutch astronomer Christiaan Huygens who first clearly saw Saturn's ring system and announced its discovery. And what an amazing system it is! Composed of countless chunks of water-ice and rock, the rings measure some 170,000 miles across—but are razor-thin, at less than a hundred *feet* in thickness in most places! They completely encircle Saturn's globe (around its equator), which is about 72,000 miles in diameter.

Just like Jupiter, Saturn has a large retinue of moons, numbering 62 at last count. They require a telescope to be seen—with the exception of the largest one, called *Titan*. It can be glimpsed in binoculars as a dim point of light changing position around Saturn from week to week. This moon is "supersized" for a satellite, as big as the planet Mercury! It's also unusual in having a dense atmosphere, composed mainly of methane—and also methane and brine lakes under its clouds, as discovered by the Huygens probe sent to its surface from the visiting Cassini spacecraft.

Saturn's moons combine with its rings to create a cosmic spectacle that occurs every 15 years. Twice during its 29.5-year orbit of the Sun, the planet presents its rings edgewise to the Earth. At such times, its satellites can be seen "threading" the thin luminous line representing the rings like moving beads on a string, as they merrily orbit the planet!

I'd like to share a closing thought here about Saturn that's often crossed my mind whenever I've looked at it. When at opposition and closest, it comes to within

750 million miles of the Earth. What if it happened to be much farther away, so much so that it might have been another century or more before we could admire its magnificent system of rings? Is it possible that our Creator placed Saturn in orbit where it is now—and at the same time gave us the discovery of that magic glass called the telescope so that we could look upon it— expressly for our viewing pleasure? Is this just another of those "coincidences," like the one involved in making a total eclipse of the Sun possible?

It almost seems to me as if the universe wants us to be in a constant state of awe—or of "radical amazement," as author Judy Cannato calls it. If that's the case, it has succeeded oh-so-wonderfully!

Uranus

Now here's a very strange world indeed. Nearly four times as big as Earth, this greenish-looking planet is tipped more than 98 degrees on its side! Obviously something cataclysmic happened to Uranus in the past. But it's not unique in that sense, as Venus is also upside down and rotates backward with respect to the Sun and the other planets.

And there's strong evidence that the Earth itself has moved on its axis over the eons—and may be in the process of getting ready to do so again. It is known that the magnetic field resulting from the Earth's iron core is already slowly moving. According to Native American belief, this will be the time of the "Great Purification" during which Mother Earth will cleanse itself—and it is said it will occur "soon." (The ultimate reference for those interested in this subject is *Pole Shift* by John White, published by A.R.E. Press.)

In the case of Uranus itself, during the course of its 84-year orbit of the Sun, we alternately see it pole-on and then on its side, since its axis (like that of the Earth and other planets) remains fixed in its direction in space. Despite its average distance of *1.7 billion* miles from us, it is faintly visible to the unaided eye on a dark, moonless night, as long as you know when and where to look in the sky! (*Sky & Telescope* should be consulted for details on its visibility.) In binoculars it appears like a greenish star (and as a tiny green pea in small telescopes).

There's a great sense of accomplishment in spotting this remote world, which was unknown throughout most of history until its discovery by William Herschel in 1781. Actually, it had been unknowingly seen over a century and a half earlier by Galileo, appearing as a background "star" in some of his sketches of Jupiter and its moons! But he didn't recognize it for what it was. Neither did Herschel initially, thinking it was a new comet.

No one had ever considered the possibility of other planets existing beyond those that had been known since antiquity. Its orbit soon indicated that it was indeed a new world! Although it moves much more slowly than any of the planets closer to the Sun, the week-to-week orbital motion of Uranus can be seen even in binoculars by comparing its place in the sky with background stars.

Neptune

Continuing our outward journey through the solar system, we come to the last of the "real" planets in the

Sun's family. (I'll explain this more fully in the section that follows, on Pluto.) At an average distance of 2.7 billion miles from Earth (that's a billion miles farther than Uranus!), this remote world can't be seen with the unaided eye. But it can be spotted with binoculars, appearing as a very dim bluish star. (Again, check *Sky & Telescope*.) Its nickname is Big Blue, since its dense atmosphere appears distinctly bluish in Hubble Space Telescope images, in contrast to Uranus's obvious greenish one. Almost exactly four times the size of the Earth, Neptune is nearly a twin of Uranus except for differences in temperature (and to some extent in atmospheric composition) at their extreme distances—19 times that of Earth from the Sun in the case of Uranus and 30 times in the case of Neptune!

It should be mentioned that both planets have very faint systems of rings and retinues of satellites, but these lie far beyond the range of binoculars (and small telescopes as well). Neptune itself requires 165 years to complete one orbit of the Sun and was first found in 1846. (Its discovery resulted from a complex interplay of calculation and observation involving astronomers in France, Germany, and England.)

And here's a final fascinating fact concerning Neptune that surprises (and confuses) many people: During part of its orbit, it actually reigns as the outermost planet! This is due to Pluto's highly eccentric orbit (see the next section), which brings it inside Neptune's for several years at a time. But in any case, Big Blue marks the official outer edge of the solar system as far as major planets are concerned.

Pluto & Beyond

In 1930, the world was electrified by the announce-
ment from the Lowell Observatory in Arizona that a
ninth planet had been discovered there. (The discoverer, Clyde Tombaugh, had originally been an amateur astronomer who observed the planets using a homemade
reflecting telescope, and his sketches brought him to the
attention of the observatory and resulted in a position
there.) Lying at an average distance from us of 3.6 billion
miles, Pluto is so remote that it takes 248 years to circle
the Sun once and appears as only a very faint star even
in large observatory telescopes.

But then just a few years ago it happened: The International Astronomical Union (the official worldwide
organization of professional astronomers) made head-
lines at one of their meetings by demoting Pluto from its
status as a full-fledged planet to that of a minor planet
or a "plutoid"! Many people were (and still are) unhappy
with that decision, including lots of astronomers I know.
However, there were reasons for this drastic action. It
turns out that recent observations show that Pluto is actually *smaller than our Moon*—not much of a planet at all!

Additionally, Pluto has a very strange orbit that's
highly inclined to the plane of the solar system (the
ecliptic), unlike those of all the other planets. Many astronomers believe that Pluto was originally a satellite
of either Neptune or Uranus that somehow got torn
away—possibly accounting for why the latter planet is
flipped over on its side. And finally, observers have now
found a host of ice-ball worlds like Pluto out beyond it,
a number of which are bigger than it is! These bodies
are "leftovers" from the birth of the solar system some

4.6 billion years ago and occupy a region known as the *Kuiper Belt.* The larger of these collectively may account for the persistent evidence of the existence of a tenth planet (or "Planet X," as it's often referred to), affecting the orbits of Uranus and Neptune.

So poor, once-proud Pluto—along with its system of five small satellites—has now been relegated to being a minor member of our planetary system. As I've mentioned before, it often happens that advances in astronomy and related sciences, as important as they are in expanding our understanding of the universe, take away some of its romance and mystery. The fanciful ideas of seas on the Moon and canals on Mars are just two examples that come immediately to mind. As a confessed romantic myself, I do miss them!

CHAPTER 10

COMETS, METEORS & ASTEROIDS

The Major "Impact" of Minor Bodies

Wrapping up the solar system, we now survey its lesser—but still vitally important—members.

Comets

Far out beyond Pluto and its ice-ball cousins lies an enormous halo of comets known as the *Oort Cloud.* Like the minor planets, these objects are the remnants of the vast nebula of gas, dust, and ice from which the solar system originally formed some 4.6 billion years ago. And it's estimated that there may be *millions* of them residing in the dim twilight out there! (The actual process by which they were created is somewhat shrouded in mystery, but essentially ice and dust coalesced around rocky material, which itself had condensed from the solar nebula.)

We've all seen pictures of comets trailing long, graceful tails. But the tails only appear when they head inward toward the Sun in their highly elliptical orbits and its heat evaporates the ices from the nucleus of the comet itself. During most of their orbit, they are essentially "dirty ice balls," as astronomers refer to them. The tail typically grows longer the closer the comet comes to the Sun. And while some tails have stretched over 100 million miles in length (greater than the Earth–Sun distance!), they are essentially a vacuum. Indeed, when famed Halley's Comet appeared in 1910, its graceful tail swept across the Earth with no measureable effect! Despite sensitive scientific observations made around the world looking for it, no trace of the tail was found.

Another interesting fact about comet tails: They always point away from the direction of the Sun, since its radiation pressure spawns them. (It's the pressure exerted by this so-called solar wind that's behind plans to send ships "coasting" to the stars, using huge sails pushed by sunlight.) This means that when coming inward, the tail trails the head of the comet, as we're all used to seeing. But after the comet rounds the Sun and heads back out to where it came from, *it goes tail-first!* As I mentioned, many comets have elliptical orbits—like that of Halley, which takes 76 years to circle the Sun and last retuned to our skies in 1986. However, others have an open-ended hyperbolic orbit, indicating they are visiting the Sun only once and then heading out into interstellar space to find another star!

Comets are named after their discoverers, and until recently many were found by amateur astronomers sweeping the sky purposefully for them. (The famed stargazer Leslie Peltier, who is profiled in the final chapter, found a dozen of them during his lifetime!) But sadly, today automated sky surveys at major observatories are finding most of them. Still, a few continue to be spotted by backyard stargazers—and not always using a telescope. Some of the brighter ones have actually been found with binoculars!

Whether or not you set out to "ride a comet to fame," these objects are often a spectacle to behold. There have been those like Comet Hale-Bopp (named after its two discoverers) in 1997, which was an amazing sight as seen with the unaided eye for many months! And you just never know when a spectacular new comet will grace the nighttime skies. The best way to keep abreast of both returning and newly discovered comets is to check *Sky & Telescope* or *Astronomy* (for the very latest information, look at their websites).

In ages past, comets were regarded as omens portending both bad and good news—the deaths of kings, the births of princes, battles lost and won, and similar events happening around their appearance as bright, naked-eye spectacles in the sky. But today they are objects of wonder and awe.

And they have taken on a profound and unexpected status. It's now believed that these giant balls of mostly frozen water were largely responsible for creating the oceans of the Earth from repeated impacts with it during its early history. Moreover, *the carbon compounds contained in their nuclei may well have had something to do with the seeding of life itself on our planet!* The theory is that these molecules formed the basic building blocks of life—driven by sunlight and immersed in the primordial "soup" of the early oceans.

Meteors

As a comet enters the inner solar system, material is driven off its head by radiation pressure from the Sun, combined with gravitational effects of the planets, and is scattered along its path. When our Spaceship Earth in its 66,000-mile-per-hour orbit crosses these paths, pieces of this material enter our atmosphere and burn up from friction—creating what is popularly called a *shooting star.* Technically, these are known as *meteors,* while those pieces that survive their fiery plunge and reach the ground are called *meteorites.* Meteors typically range from the size of sand grains to that of a pea or a walnut. Bigger but rarer ones known as *fireballs* can light up the landscape and leave sonic booms in their wake as they cross the sky in a matter of seconds!

Small meteorites that fit in your hand are often sold in mineral and gem stores, while enormous masses weighing many *tons* are displayed in planetariums and science museums. Whatever its size, a meteorite gives you an opportunity to "touch a piece of heaven"! It will also be the oldest thing you'll ever put your hands on, with most of them dated at 4.6 billion years (the age of the solar system).

And here's another thing to consider: Meteorites are "extraterrestrials" in the truest sense of the word (they are not of the Earth!). I sometimes bait my lecture audiences by promising to introduce them to an extraterrestrial at the end of the program—whereupon I whip out my walnut-size meteorite (and if the group isn't too large, pass it around for them to actually touch).

If moonlight doesn't interfere, meteors can be seen in the sky on any clear night—at the rate of about one every five minutes or so on average. (But unlike most other celestial objects, they are *not* well suited for meditation. Seeing one is an exhilarating and jolting experience!) Most of these are rather faint and are called *sporadic meteors*, because they appear randomly around the sky, coming from no specific direction.

In contrast, *meteor showers* are concentrated displays of dozens to nearly a hundred shooting stars per hour appearing to radiate from a particular constellation (after which they are named). Of the major annual showers, two of the best are the *Perseids*, which reach peak activity on the night of August 11–12; and the *Geminids* on December 13–14. Under a dark sky (again, no moonlight and little or no light pollution), upwards of a hundred per hour can be seen on these nights.

Even more dramatic than a meteor shower is a *meteor storm*. When such an event happens, we're talking about *thousands* of shooting stars per hour! But meteor storms are very unpredictable. The most famous of these are the *Leonids*, which typically peak on the night of November 16–17. Normally, a modest 15 to 20 meteors an hour will be seen. But occasionally, and almost always unpredictably, the sky is filled with shooting stars radiating from the constellation of Leo.

There's nothing quite so relaxing or as exciting as a meteor watch. And this is one area of stargazing where the unaided eye, with its "all-sky" viewing capability, reigns supreme! Here's how to go about it.

EXERCISE:
Meteor Watch

- Recline comfortably on a lawn chair or sleeping bag, facing in the direction of the shower's radiant (the constellation it's named for) and concentrating overhead to get optimum coverage of the meteors as they spread out across the sky. Don't forget to bring a blanket and a thermos of something hot to drink—it gets cold lying outside late at night!

- Notice that the later you stay up, the more meteors you see. (This is because before midnight, we're on the side of the Earth facing away from the direction the meteors are coming, and they have to "catch up" with us. After midnight we're turned in the direction of the Earth's orbital motion, and the meteors slam into the atmosphere at higher speeds, resulting not only in more meteors being seen but also in them appearing brighter.)

  Some meteors may display color, depending on their speed and composition (which includes iron, nickel, glass, and rock). For any given shower, the radiant itself may be below the horizon at the time you venture outdoors, and meteors will be seen streaming over it. As the evening progresses, the radiant climbs ever higher in the sky due to the Earth spinning eastward.

- Here's a special treat: As you look from time to time directly at the radiant itself, you may suddenly see a point of light appear, get rapidly brighter and brighter, and then vanish. This is a shooting star "shooting" directly at you!

- Finally, if you have binoculars, do bring them along. Many meteors leave "trains" or trails behind them that persist for several seconds after the meteor itself disintegrates (often in a burst of light!) and disappears. While following a meteor in binoculars is typically very difficult since they move so rapidly, watching their trains dissipate in these glasses is a fascinating activity.

On a November morning just before dawn in 1966, I (and most of the worldwide astronomical community wherever it was still dark) was totally blown away when the Leonids unexpectedly reached a rate of *40 meteors per second* (or 144,000 per hour) and looked like snowflakes coming at you in a driving snowstorm! There have been other Leonid storms since, but none to date have matched that amazing display. (Outbursts similar to the 1966 one were seen in 1799, 1833, and 1866. During the 1833 display, many people actually feared that the world was coming to an end!)

Asteroids

Between the orbits of Mars and Jupiter is a vast region of cosmic rubble known as the *asteroid zone*. More than a million objects have been found there to date, ranging from boulder-size chunks up to the "big four" bodies: Pallas, Vesta, Juno, and Ceres. The last of these measures nearly 500 miles in diameter.

Also known as "minor planets," they're thought to represent material that never had a chance to form a full-fledged planet—or, more likely, to be the remains of a planet that once existed but disintegrated for some reason (possibly a collision with an interloper into the solar system?). Interestingly, in one of Edgar Cayce's readings, the psychic said that "there is missing some one of the Earth's companions or planets, and the combustion or destruction of same caused much changes." Whichever explanation is correct, asteroids have had a profound effect on the Earth over the eons.

It's now widely agreed that an asteroid impact is what took out the dinosaurs some 65 million years ago and caused other mass extinctions on our planet. There's even some evidence that it was a massive asteroid or comet nucleus that split apart the huge supercontinent Gondwanaland. Although most of these objects stay within the asteroid zone itself, perturbations resulting from gravitational influences of the planets (especially from massive Jupiter) regularly cause a few of them to wander toward the inner planets—including Mars and the Earth.

Astronomers (and geologists) have only recently begun waking up to the fact that we are continually under bombardment, and there are now several NASA-sponsored projects using highly specialized telescopes to monitor the sky for incoming "near-Earth asteroids" or "near-Earth objects," as they are referred to by scientists. There have been a number of spectacular close calls within the past several years. One of these involved an object traveling at 40,000 miles per hour that came *ten times closer to us than the Moon* in 2010! Another came within 17,000 miles in February 2013. It's sobering to think that most, if not all, life on this planet might have perished in an instant had these stray asteroids impacted the Earth.

Detecting a threatening asteroid is one thing—diverting or destroying it in time is another. But plans are being considered to do just that. In any case, here's yet another reason to follow the oft-given advice *Carpe diem*—to live each day to the fullest. But who would have ever thought we would have a cosmic reason for doing so?

For the casual stargazer, the four largest asteroids can be followed in binoculars (and when Ceres is closest to us, with the unaided eye as well). They appear as dim points of light slowly moving from hour to hour against the starry background. *Astronomy* and *Sky & Telescope* both regularly alert readers to their visibility when within range. There have been several spacecraft missions sent for close-up looks at asteroids (and comets as well), and oh, how differently they appear than in binoculars! Their surfaces are covered with craters and fractures, the evident scars of their violent origin. Some of them even have smaller bodies orbiting them like little moons.

Asteroids were unknown until the year 1800, when Ceres was discovered. Today they are among the hottest and most critically important topics in all of solar-system astronomy. And aside from potential impacts with the Earth, they are believed to contain many valuable minerals. As a result, plans are already on the drawing board for commercial ventures to go and mine them as replacements for dwindling resources on our own planet.

And now, our journey continues—as we plunge into the vastness of the cosmic ocean and the "great beyond" in Part IV!

PART IV

WONDERS OF DEEP SPACE

CHAPTER 11

STELLAR BEACONS

Stars as Suns

If the solar system alone had been the limits of cosmic creation, it would still have filled us with an unending sense of awe, wonder, and mystery. But it is only a single drop in the celestial ocean. In taking leave of our Sun and its family, we now approach even more amazing scenes of inexpressible grandeur. We are to contemplate not one sun, but thousands, millions, and even billions of them! As I stated earlier, our Sun is a star—and the stars are other suns. There are superdense ones smaller than our Moon, while some supergiant suns are big enough to contain our entire solar system within them.

And the sheer number of stars is totally mind-blowing. It's been repeatedly shown (statistically, using supercomputers) that *there are more stars within reach of today's largest telescopes than all of the grains of sand on all of the beaches and deserts on the entire Earth!*

And this host of heaven is bound by the same universal law of gravitation that holds a pebble to the ground, guides a falling raindrop, or keeps the Moon and planets in their orbits. What, we may ask, *is* gravitation? It remains one of the greatest mysteries of science. (But perhaps the visionary Buckminster Fuller gave us a clue in his book *Critical Path* when he said, "Love is metaphysical gravity.")

The Assembled Starlords

American writer and stargazer Charles Edward Barns waxed poetic in his long-out-of-print observing classic *1001 Celestial Wonders:* "Lo, the Star-Lords are assembling. And the banquet-board is set. We approach with fear and trembling. But we leave them with regret."

The thousands of stars visible to the unaided eye on a clear night are arranged on an apparent brightness or "magnitude" scale created by early skywatchers, with the faintest ones being rated 6th-magnitude and the brightest ones 1st-magnitude. Astronomers later found that there's actually quite a range of brightness among the latter stars, so the scale was expanded to 0-magnitude and then to negative values. Sirius, the brightest of all the stars, is assigned a magnitude of –1.4.

(Extending the scale further, the major planets are even brighter—with Venus as the brightest of them, peaking at magnitude –4.4, the Moon when full at –12.7, and the Sun at –26.8. Going in the opposite direction, astronomers are now studying galaxies at the edge of the observable universe as faint as +26th-magnitude and even beyond.)

The very brightest stars spread all over the entire heavens (both Northern and Southern Hemispheres) belong to an exclusive stellar fraternity, the "First-Magnitude Club." It's these gems (and their host constellations) that are easiest to become intimate "friends" with, due to their prominence in the sky. These are also the stars most suited for meditation in their role as celestial mandalas, as discussed in Chapter 3. They display an amazing array of heavenly hues, their colors primarily reflecting their temperatures—hot stars being bluish and cool ones reddish. (Star color is not an indication of composition, as is usually assumed: stars are made nearly entirely of hydrogen, plus some helium and various trace elements.)

Stars are generally designated by a Greek letter in order of brightness within their constellation, followed by that group's Latin possessive name. Many of the brighter ones, including all those in the "club," also have proper names. So the brightest star in Orion, *Betelgeuse,* is also known as Alpha Orionis, and the second brightest, *Rigel,* is Beta Orionis.

The roster on the following page contains 17 of my favorite luminaries, together with their host constellation, brightness, perceived hue, and distance in light-years (see the next section for an explanation of this term). Note that a few have a magnitude range given, indicating that they change in brightness. Such objects will be discussed in the next chapter, on variable stars. All of these gems can be found plotted and named on the *Sky & Telescope* and *Astronomy* monthly star maps (and also on most rotating star charts), making it easy to identify them in the sky.

NAME	CONSTELLATION	MAGNITUDE	COLOR	DISTANCE (LY)
Sirius	Canis Major	−1.4	bluish-white	8.6
Arcturus	Bootes	0.0	golden-topaz	37
Vega	Lyra	0.0	pale-sapphire	25
Capella	Auriga	0.1	golden-yellow	42
Rigel	Orion	0.2	bluish-white	770
Procyon	Canis Minor	0.4	yellowish-white	11
Betelgeuse	Orion	0.4–1.3	ruddy-orange	520
Altair	Aquila	0.8	bluish-white	17
Aldebaran	Taurus	0.8–1.0	rosy-topaz	65
Antares	Scorpius	1.0–1.8	fiery-red	600
Spica	Virgo	1.0	icy-blue	260
Pollux	Gemini	1.2	yellowish-orange	34
Fomalhaut	Piscis Austrinus	1.2	bluish-white	25
Deneb	Cygnus	1.3	bluish-white	2,300
Regulus	Leo	1.4	white	77
Adhara	Canis Major	1.5	bluish-white	490
Castor	Gemini	1.6	bluish-white	52

The Light-Year

Astronomical distances are so vast compared to those on our earthly abode that astronomers use a special yardstick called the *light-year*. It's the distance a beam of light travels over the course of a year, moving at a speed of 186,000 miles per second. To put the speed of light itself in perspective, if you turned on a flashlight and the light could bend, it would circle the Earth seven times in just one second! Pointing your flashlight at the Moon, its light would reach there in less than two seconds; at the Sun, in eight minutes; and at Pluto, in about five hours.

In a single year, light travels nearly *six trillion* (6,000,000,000,000) miles! Such a huge number is totally meaningless to us. We can walk a few miles, drive a few hundred, fly a few thousand—but when it comes to millions, billions, and trillions of miles, forget it!

Well, here's an amazing fact that will hopefully help you comprehend the immensity of this unit: If you were to start counting the number of miles in a light-year at the rate of one mile per second, it would take you *150,000 years* to count up to six trillion! And this is the astronomer's standard "yardstick" for measuring cosmic distances!

There's no star within a light-year of us (except our Sun); the nearest is the Alpha Centauri system, at 4.3 light-years (or 7,000 times as distant as Pluto). And we are now observing galaxies and quasars with the Hubble Space Telescope and other large instruments out to ranges of nearly 14 billion light-years.

Meditative Moment

What boundary may ultimately be set to creation we don't know, but we can trace it sufficiently to perceive that as far as our senses are concerned, it can't be distinguished from absolute infinity. To some people, contemplating such immensity and our smallness within it is actually frightening. But this shouldn't be so. The real wonder here is that within the confines of our tiny brains we can contemplate such vastness at all.

This proves to me beyond any doubt that our minds are patterned after the "Great Mind" behind all of creation. Remember, also, as we discussed in Chapter 3, daunting as cosmic distances may seem, our minds can go anywhere in the universe <u>*instantly at the speed of thought!*</u> *And sometimes our souls may go there, too.*

Time-Traveling Across Space

Astronomers are often referred to as "time travelers" for the simple (but profound!) reason that *the farther out you look into space, the further back into time you are seeing.* Indeed, images of the entire history of the Earth, beginning with its birth in the solar nebula 4.6 billion years ago and all periods in between then and now, are traveling outward at the speed of light.

I like to think that someday we will meet advanced beings from distant space who will play back for us those parts of our history that have reached them at their respective distances from us. This presupposes, of course, that they will have the ability to somehow "time-jump" to our present! And why not? As the celebrated writer Arthur C. Clarke stated in one of his famous dictums, "Any sufficiently advanced technology will be indistinguishable from magic." (Just imagine someone from, say, the Middle Ages being shown any of our modern technological marvels. Talk about culture shock!)

Telescopes make it possible to look out into space billions of light-years (and therefore back into time billions of years). And even using just binoculars, galaxies millions of light-years away can be seen. (As I'll discuss in Chapter 17, it's actually possible to glimpse the Andromeda Galaxy without optical aid at a distance of some 2.4 million light-years!) With the unaided eye, stars can be seen out to several thousand light-years.

EXERCISE:
Meditating Upon a Star

- First, identify stars from the roster of stellar luminaties (see page 138) that are visible at the time you are observing the sky (two of summer and two from winter have been selected for illustration here).

- Begin by looking at Vega in Lyra and ask yourself: What were you doing when the light you see tonight left this beautiful sapphire gem 25 summers ago? (The assumption is that you *were* on the planet then! If not, what do you think your parents or an older sibling was doing then?)

- Then switch to the super-sun Deneb (60,000 times as luminous as our Sun!) in nearby Cygnus. Its light left there 2,300 years ago, prior to the birth of Christianity. What do you suppose was happening here on Earth 23 centuries ago?

- Gaze in wonder at the radiant diamond Sirius in Canis Major, brightest of all the stars! The light you're seeing left this star just about nine years ago. Being so brief a time, it should be easy to contemplate significant events that occurred in your life back then.

- Look at ruddy Betelgeuse in Orion. Its light left the star 520 years ago, around the time Columbus discovered America. Can you picture what our world was like during this first Age of Exploration (long before the Space Age)?

  In each case, as you stare at the star, realize that archaic photons are entering your eyes and ending their long journey across interstellar space and time on your retinas. You are in *direct physical contact* with that distant sun through the amazing "photon connection" discussed in Chapter 3. Oh, how glorious to simply meditate upon a star!

Other Solar Systems: Planets Everywhere!

Considering that stars are suns and our Sun is a star, it seems reasonable that they should have systems of planets orbiting them, just as ours does. That was long the speculation, but there wasn't any way to verify this until the advances of modern astronomy.

Theories of how stars are born had indicated that as a spinning protostar condensed out of its gaseous womb, it would spin faster and faster—and if it didn't somehow slow down its spin, it would eventually tear itself apart. A good analogy here is that of a spinning ice-skater. As she pulls her arms closer in toward her body, she spins faster and faster. Her spin is slowed and finally stopped by extending her arms. The baby star slows its spin by shedding rings of material, which act as stellar "brake shoes." That material in turn condenses into planets! So it appeared that a star would have to have planets as part of its birth process.

But that was only theory. Confirmation was a long time coming, but come it did—employing three different, independent observational techniques (the *astrometric, spectroscopic,* and *photometric* methods). Using the last of these, the orbiting Kepler observatory alone has discovered *thousands* of planetary systems surrounding stars in just a relatively small area of the summer Milky Way that it's monitoring. Even more exciting is that hundreds of these planets are located in the stars' so-called Goldilocks zone. This is the region surrounding them where it's neither "too hot" nor "too cold"—just right for water to exist in the liquid state. And this raises the thrilling possibility (some exobiologists say *certainty*) that life exists there.

The three methods mentioned are all considered "indirect" since they don't actually let you see the planet itself but only its effect on its sun. This is because these worlds are typically billions of times fainter than the parent stars whose light they reflect. Applying state-of-the-art electro-optical technology to huge optical telescopes has finally made it possible to image some of these planets directly. What an amazing technological feat this is!

Revelations of Starlight

I must now tell you of another, much earlier achievement concerning the stars that is truly a triumph of the human mind. Other than measuring a star's brightness and position in the sky (and in some cases its distance by trigonometric triangulation—see the next section), many noted astronomers and philosophers of centuries past went on record as saying that we could never learn anything about the actual physical nature of a remote sun. (To me, this smacks of peremptory statements like "man can't fly" and other such dismissive pontifications from on high. My favorite one is the remark by the Astronomer Royal of England that spaceflight "is utter bilge," made just prior to the surprise launching of Sputnik!)

But apparently the Creator of the Universe had other ideas! Not only were we given the gift of the telescope itself, but also the gift of the colorful spectrum seen when sunlight passes through a glass prism (or through a raindrop in the case of a rainbow). Using an instrument called the *spectrograph,* modern astronomers can not only analyze the composition of a star—but also its size, temperature, mass, density, and age; how fast it spins; its velocity through space; and many other physical parameters!

How magical and wonderful! As the French physicist and Nobel laureate Jean Perrin said: "It is indeed a feeble light that reaches us from the starry sky. But what would human thought have achieved if we could not see the stars?"

How Do We Know That?

In closing this chapter, I want to answer a question that may well be on your mind right now, as it frequently is for those in my lecture audiences: Just how can we *really* know for sure even the most basic facts about a remote star, such as its distance from us? Well, depending on the type of object involved—a planet, star, nebula, galaxy, or whatever the case may be—there are as many as a dozen different independent methods of determining how far away it is. And let me show you through a simple experiment one of the most basic of these.

Please close one of your eyes (doesn't matter which one) and put a finger up against your nose. Notice where it appears in relation to the room you're in. Next, switch eyes—open the one that was closed and close the one that was open. You'll see that your finger has now shifted its position against the room. That shift is known as *parallax,* and it results from viewing your finger from two different directions (the space between your eyes). Finally, hold your finger at the end of your arm, and switch your eyes back and forth again. Your finger still shifts, but not as much. In other words, the farther something is from you, the smaller its parallax.

This is the same method that surveyors traditionally used to measure the distance across a lake, for example—by taking sightings of an object on the other side from two different positions along the shore. The triangle thus formed could then easily be solved for the distance by basic trigonometry. (Today they use laser rangers!)

Applied to the stars, blinking your eyes will show no shift—nor would sightings even taken from opposite sides of the Earth's 8,000-mile diameter—because the stars are simply too far away! But guess what astronomers came up with to get a big enough baseline? They image a star, say, tonight . . . and then wait six months. By then the Earth has moved to the other side of its orbit, nearly 200 million miles from where the first picture was taken. Reimaging the star reveals a small but *directly measurable* parallax, and thus its distance. Very clever!

This chapter has discussed single stable stars—ones like our own Sun. But many stars are unstable, pulsating like giant beating hearts and, in some cases, actually exploding! We examine these "restless" suns next. . . .

CHAPTER 12

VARIABLE & EXPLODING STARS

Restless Suns

Variable stars are the surprise packages of the universe! Some 10 percent of all stars change in brightness with time—some over a period of hours or days, others over months or years.

Variability is an indication of instability. And this happens both at the beginning of a star's life and again at its end. Baby stars are formed by condensing from the beautiful clouds of hydrogen gas and dust known as *nebulae*. These stellar nurseries are often shown in spectacular photos from the Hubble Space Telescope and other big scopes. Although this process takes millions of years to complete (a relatively brief time, cosmically speaking, in a star's multibillion-year life span), when the temperature and pressure are just right for the onset of thermonuclear reactions, the star begins to shine. And this happens in *just three minutes!*

Then, as the star approaches the waning years of its long life, it again becomes unstable and begins ejecting its outer layers—returning the material it's made from back out into space, where it originated. Eventually, the star as we knew it "dies." Many are both surprised and saddened to learn that stars die, for they seem eternal compared to our brief human lifetimes. But there is no reason for regret: *from the ashes of the dying stars, the new stars are formed!* (And as we'll see later in this chapter, the core of the star itself still exists!) Believers in past lives, including followers of Edgar Cayce and his many readings on the subject, would likely refer to this recycling process as "stellar reincarnation," which in a sense it actually *is.*

Mira, the Wonder Star

There are no variable stars visible to the unaided eye in the case of their birth, given they incubate within tight cocoons of gas and dust that largely hide the star until it's born. (As I mentioned, the nebulae themselves from which they condense are quite obvious and beautiful as seen in telescopes and photographs.) But the long road to the stellar graveyard is another story.

A mature star that's been shining in most cases for billions of years becomes unstable and begins to pulsate like some colossal cosmic beating heart. And there are hundreds of these around the sky visible to the unaided eye and in binoculars. One of the most famous is Mira (Omicron Ceti) in the constellation of Cetus, the Whale. It was, in fact, the first variable star to be recognized by early stargazers, who looked upon it as the "Wonder

Star." They watched it slowly appear from the darkness and brighten to an obvious 2nd-magnitude—then fade over a period of many months to below naked-eye visibility and completely disappear from view.

Mira has a period averaging 330 days in length and is classified as a "long-period variable." It's fun to check its location in the sky from time to time with the unaided eye. Often there's no sign of it—and then, one night a glimmer of light appears and continues to brighten noticeably from week to week. Binoculars make it possible to spot it sooner, and also to follow it long after it disappears from naked-eye visibility. In keeping with the "cosmic beating heart" analogy, Mira appears reddish throughout its cycle! It lies some 220 light-years from us in a barren-looking area of the fall sky.

Betelgeuse

Mira isn't the only reddish-looking variable star. Most of these "pulsators" are huge red supergiant suns, often exhibiting striking colors, especially as seen in binoculars and telescopes. One of the loveliest visible to the unaided eye is Betelgeuse (Alpha Orionis) in the winter constellation Orion. The ruddy-orange or topaz hue of this radiant 1st-magnitude sun is obvious at a glance, while its brightness varies by about a magnitude irregularly over a period of several years.

As you gaze upon this star, here's something to contemplate: This colossus fluctuates in size between 480 million and 800 million miles in diameter as it pulsates. And while its thermonuclear core has a temperature of millions of degrees, like those of most stars, its outer atmosphere is actually cool enough to contain water vapor (steam)! It's so huge that it also has one (and possibly two) smaller companion stars actually orbiting *within* its atmosphere! This amazing super-sun is 520 light-years distant.

Herschel's Garnet Star

An even redder star than Betelgeuse is Mu Cephei in the late summer and fall constellation, Cepheus. It's better known as Herschel's Garnet Star, after William Herschel, who first called attention to its rich red color. Varying irregularly in brightness between 3rd- and 5th-magnitude, it's visible to the unaided eye throughout its two-year cycle. But its hue is much more distinctly seen in binoculars.

This is not only one of the reddest stars known, but also one of the largest—nearly a *billion* miles in diameter! Given these facts, it's definitely worth the effort to seek out this faintish gem. As in the case of all the objects beyond the solar system discussed in this book, consult the monthly star maps in *Sky & Telescope* or *Astronomy* for its actual location in the sky. Thanks to its vast size and intrinsic brightness, Herschel's Garnet Star is one of the remotest suns visible to the unaided eye, at its distance of 2,800 light-years!

Algol, the Demon Star

Not all stars that change in brightness are real variable suns. Some are impostors! And the most famous of these is Algol (Beta Persei) in the fall and winter constellation Perseus. Ancient skywatchers saw it apparently "winking" at them every three days like clockwork and called it the Demon Star. Normally shining at a constant 2nd-magnitude, suddenly over a period of just ten hours Algol dims to 3rd-magnitude and then reverts back to its original brightness. People were understandably mystified by this behavior, and centuries were to pass before an explanation was given.

Algol consists of two suns closely orbiting each other, one much dimmer than the other. (Double stars are very numerous and will be explored in the next chapter.) But what makes such "eclipsing binaries" unique is that *their orbits are presented edgewise* to us here on Earth. As one star passes in front of the other, it eclipses it and causes a drop in its brightness. To see this for yourself, consult *Sky & Telescope* or *Astronomy* for the dates and times of the eclipses (which are given when Perseus is well placed for evening viewing).

Meditative Moment

To watch Algol wink, go out several hours before the actual time of minimum light and compare its brightness to that of the nearby star Mirfak (Alpha Persei), which shines at a steady 2nd-magnitude. Realize that you are witnessing the mutual revolution of two suns far out in the depths of interstellar space with nothing more than the unaided eye! Now just how amazing is that? And you're watching their antics from a distance of over 100 light-years.

Novae & Supernovae

Most stars age gracefully (and beautifully, as we'll see when discussing the nebulae and the amazing cosmic "artwork" and "sculptures" they create, in Chapter 15). But there are exceptions, for the rare "heavyweight" stars go out with a bang and explode violently on their way to the stellar graveyard. The *novae* are less violent and more common than are the *supernovae,* which are among the most massive and luminous stars in the universe and relatively rare. (There are also the *recurrent novae,* which are stars that erupt more than once.)

The actual astrophysics involved for the various types is quite complex and outside the scope of this book. Suffice it to say that the sudden appearance of a bright "new" star (thus the origin of the name *nova*) in the sky can be quite exciting. But rather than being a true new star, it's actually an old one in its death throes. Hundreds are on record, and a new nova bright enough to be seen with the unaided eye appears every few years or so. But only a handful of supernovae have ever been seen over the centuries (other than ones in other galaxies).

The three brightest and most famous of these are those of A.D. 1054 in Taurus (seen by Chinese astronomers and which produced the famed Crab Nebula); of 1572 in Cassiopeia, seen by Tycho Brahe (Tycho's Star); and of 1604 in Ophiuchus, observed by Johannes Kepler (Kepler's Star). In the latter two cases at least, the stars were brighter than Venus and visible in broad daylight—finally fading from view after more than a year.

A nova may appear unexpectedly at any time, and once familiar with the constellations, you should always give the sky a careful "once-over" when you venture out on clear nights scanning for any bright star that seems out of place and "shouldn't be there." Automated patrols by professional astronomers find most of them today, but some are still first reported by amateurs who know the sky well. And we are way overdue for the next supernova to appear. Should you be the first to report it, you'll achieve instant international "stardom"!

And Southern Hemisphere readers take note: The erratic star Eta Carinae in the fall (for you) constellation Carina may be ready to go supernova at any time, according to some astronomers. It's at the heart of the majestic Eta Carinae Nebula, which is some four full-Moon diameters in apparent size and readily visible to the unaided eye. Eta itself is considered intrinsically one of the most luminous and massive suns in our galaxy. It has appeared as bright as 2nd-magnitude in the past—and once in the mid-1800s briefly became one of the brightest stars in the entire sky! It currently slumbers restlessly between 4th- and 6th-magnitude, and could awaken on the next clear night!

I've previously pointed out that we're children of the stars—that we're literally made of stardust! Here's why:

When a star goes supernova, it "seeds" the gas and dust of the interstellar medium with the heavier elements necessary for life. The calcium in your fingernails, teeth, and bones; the iron coursing through your bloodstream right now; the carbon that makes up all of your cells; and even the potassium in your brain so you can read and understand this book were all forged within an exploding star's thermonuclear core eons ago. It's now believed that the Sun itself is at least a *third-generation star*—containing elements "cooked" in the death throes of at least two previous supermassive suns! (As Whitman said in *Leaves of Grass:* "Immense have been the preparations for me.")

Here's an interesting aside involving these unstable stars: As I've previously mentioned, the brightest star in the sky is radiant, bluish-white Sirius in Canis Major. But there are accounts in antiquity that it *used to be red!* Sirius has a small, very dense white-dwarf companion visible in telescopes. And white dwarfs are one of the end-products of a nova explosion. Could it be that this degenerate star was once a brilliant red supergiant that outshone Sirius itself?

Current theories of stellar evolution say it's impossible for a star to evolve so quickly like that in just a few centuries. But can we really be so sure? If only we had a time machine to go back to see for ourselves!

The Star of Bethlehem

One of the most famous stars in all of history is surely the Star of Bethlehem, also known as the Christmas Star. Speculating on its identity has long been a staple of planetarium shows around the world during the holiday season, and likely you've seen one of these programs yourself. There have been various theories put forth to explain it—including a bright meteor (or *bolide*), a great comet, a triple conjunction of planets, a UFO, and a supernova. Attempting to take into account uncertainties in time (the exact date of Christ's birth) and terminology (any bright object in the sky was apt to be called a "star" back then) is tricky at best.

As a longtime planetarium director myself, I've always favored the supernova theory (next to that of a moving, hovering UFO, of course!). The search is on for the remnant of such an explosion, the shards of nebulosity expanding outward from the dying star itself, which might have occurred around the time of Christ's birth. (Incidentally, as I've alluded to before, I consider myself a "Cosmic Christian," one whose God is the God of the Universe—of an infinity of worlds and not just our own small troubled planet.)

White Dwarfs, Neutron Stars & Black Holes

Much has been written in the popular literature about these bizarre stellar remnants, and they have been the subject of many television documentaries. In essence, a star becomes unstable toward the end of its life when the balance between its gravity and radiation can no longer be maintained. The stellar core begins to collapse, and its outer layers are spewed out into space.

An average star with a mass about that of our Sun will end up as a *white dwarf*. This is a star the size of the Earth, with its matter packed so tightly that its density is some 50 tons per cubic inch. A star much more massive than the Sun will end up as a rapidly spinning *neutron star*—which is an entire sun compressed into something on the order of ten miles across and having a density approaching a *million* tons per cubic inch. And the most massive stars eventually collapse in upon themselves and become *black holes*. These bizarre objects reach densities of as much as a *billion* tons per cubic inch! So dense are they, in fact, that they warp space and time around them, as Albert Einstein predicted they must.

In discussing black holes here, we're referring to *stellar-mass* ones having the mass of several Suns like ours compressed into something the size of a city block! It turns out that there are also colossal *galactic-mass* black holes at the centers of most galaxies, including our own Milky Way. These beasts have masses of *millions of Suns!*

But back to "normal" black holes. It's widely believed that the matter sucked into them ends up going through a "wormhole" (as they are called) and ends up in some other place and also at some other time! These may well be the "subways in the sky" that science-fiction writers have long dreamed and written about. Even the great rocket scientist Wernher von Braun admitted later in his life that there has to be a faster way to travel to the stars than blasting our way through space with conventional rockets. Black-hole "transit systems" spread throughout the galaxy may indeed be that way.

You may protest, "Impossible! You would be crushed out of existence if you entered one of them!" Yes, likely so. But a fascinating discovery has been made concerning these cosmic vacuum cleaners: right on the axis of a spinning black hole is a central "eye of calm" like that in a hurricane. Using this, would it be possible for us to someday, somehow, safely travel through such a wormhole to another place and time in the universe? For now, we can only wonder. But for advanced extraterrestrials, this may be an occurrence as routine as catching a subway here on Earth!

There's another surprising recent discovery related to black holes that I referenced in Chapter 3. Radio astronomers have found evidence of a musical note emanating from some of them! And interestingly, that note is B-flat on the scale—the same one that soprano and tenor saxophones are tuned to! (As I mused earlier, perhaps God is a sax player!) Despite the violent "suction" that's always pictured for black holes, Carl Sagan felt that the scene may also be one of sublime beauty and elegance. If he is roaming the cosmos he so loved in some altered state (as I and many others believe he is), I hope he finds it to be just as he imagined.

Fascinating as they are, solitary suns are the exception, rather than the rule, of the cosmos. As we're about to see, most of the stellar population is made up of combinations of stars bound closely together by gravity.

CHAPTER 13

DOUBLE & MULTIPLE STARS

Tinted Jewels of the Sky

At least 80 percent of all stars are members of double- or multiple-sun systems—two or more stars locked in an eternal orbital embrace about one another. And these range from obvious naked-eye pairs having orbital periods of many hundreds or even thousands of years, down to ones at the limits of our largest telescopes, nearly in contact with each other and orbiting in just hours or even minutes!

But the real attraction of these stellar combos is their extreme beauty, especially as seen in binoculars and telescopes. Picture this: A rich topaz-orange star closely attended by a vivid sapphire-blue one. Or how about a ruby-red, emerald-green, and aquamarine trio of suns? These are truly the tinted jewels of the sky!

And what's really amazing here is that most, if not all, stars have planets—even in double and multiple systems. So imagine living in one of them having two, three, or more suns all shining different colors in the sky instead of just our single yellowish-white Sun. Such alien landscapes actually exist in profusion throughout the universe, and other beings are surely enjoying spectacles like these on other worlds as you read this.

And contrasting colors are not the sole attraction of these gems. The members of many pairs are of the same hue, including diamond-like blue-white or dim ruby-red couplets. And there's a seemingly endless variety of differences in brightness and separations between components, as well as their positions with respect to each other, with the result that no two systems are exactly alike in appearance.

The following are just a few of the best-known and easiest-to-observe double and multiple stars.

Mizar & Alcor

The Big Dipper is familiar to just about anyone who looks skyward on spring evenings. It consists of four stars in its bowl and three in its handle. Look closely at the middle star where the handle bends, and you will see that it has a fainter companion. The primary star is Mizar, and the companion Alcor. The pair was supposedly a test for good vision in ancient times, but it's obvious to anyone having normal eyesight today. In high-powered, steadily held binoculars (or a low-power telescope), Mizar itself will be seen to consist of two stars in close proximity—one fainter than the other. All three suns are blue-white in hue.

Additionally, observations with professional instruments revealed long ago that each of these stars is itself an ultra-close binary. Thus, we are actually seeing a sextuple stellar system when we look at the middle star in the Big Dipper's handle! Mizar and Alcor are relatively nearby (astronomically speaking) at a distance of just 78 light-years from us.

Magnificent Albireo

The double star that's generally considered to be the most beautiful in the entire sky is Albireo (Beta Cygni) in the constellation Cygnus. The group itself is pictured as a graceful swan flying across the heavens, but it's actually better known as the Northern Cross. This lovely pair is the 2nd-magnitude star marking the foot of the Cross and is well placed for observation from late spring into late fall.

Viewing this wonder will require binoculars magnifying 10× or more (or a low-power telescope). As in all cases using such glasses, they must be held steadily by bracing them against something or mounting them on a tripod. (That is unless you're fortunate enough to own a pair of the wonderful but expensive image-stabilized binoculars mentioned in Chapter 5, which completely eliminate the jitters!)

Albireo features contrasting heavenly hues: a rich topaz-orange primary star with a vivid sapphire-blue companion! Some of the superlatives culled from my personal observing log from viewing this duo over the years are: "Thrilling!" "Splendid!" "Dazzling!" "Exquisite!" "Extraordinary!" "Amazing!" "Radiant!" "Glorious!" These are from its telescopic appearance, but you can still get a sense of its rare beauty in binoculars.

It's often been said that you can't call yourself a stargazer until you've seen Albireo. So put it near the top of your "must-see" list of celestial wonders! (My own "bucket list" appears in Appendix B. Most of the entries are visible to the unaided eye.) We gaze upon it from across 380 light-years of space against a rich backdrop of the summer Milky Way.

Algiedi

Here's a neat pair of orange stars easily resolved with the naked eye and a lovely sight in binoculars of all sizes. Located in the fall constellation of Capricornus, Algiedi (Alpha Capricorni) is a well-known example of an "optical double." Most double and multiple stars are real, gravitationally bound physical systems. But some are really chance alignments of unrelated stars appearing close to each other in the sky, which are actually at different distances. In the case of this combo, the brighter star lies 110 light-years from us, while the fainter one is more than six times as remote, at 700 light-years.

Herschel's Wonder Star

We now turn our attention from double to triple stars. Beta Monocerotis lies in the dim winter constellation Monoceros, and it's one of the best of its class in the sky. Although a telescope is needed to display it as the showpiece it is, binoculars will reveal an elliptical blob of white light here. This is the unresolved blended image of the three suns.

The great William Herschel was quite taken aback upon first seeing it and considered it one of the sky's stellar wonders. Should you someday get a telescope (or if you already own one), you will certainly agree with him! The distance of this stellar triple play from us is 700 light-years. It lies in the winter Milky Way (which is less obvious than the summer one).

The Double-Double

And now from triple to quadruple stars! If you look carefully at the bright summer beacon Vega in Lyra, you'll notice an elongated star near it known as Epsilon Lyrae. And should you possess excellent eyesight, it will appear as two individual points of light. Binoculars will clearly show a matched pair of white suns here. Turn a telescope at moderate magnification on them and you'll be amazed to see that each is itself a very close double star! Thus the name Double-Double. This four-star system definitely *is* real, with the one pair orbiting each other every 600 years and the other pair every 1,200 years. And, yes, the doubles themselves slowly orbit each other as well—in a period estimated at some 10,000 *centuries!*

The Trapezium

Another famous quadruple star lies embedded in heart of the beautiful Orion Nebula in the winter sky. The Nebula itself (which will be described in detail in Chapter 15) is visible to the unaided eye as a misty-looking star in the Hunter's sword, which "hangs" from his three prominent belt stars. Known as Theta-1 Orionis, this group can just barely be resolved into four stars in binoculars (depending on their magnification) and is a magnificent sight in even the smallest of telescopes, in which they appear like diamonds against green velvet!

Meditative Moment

The Trapezium is the brightest part of an actual cluster of stars that the Orion Nebula is spawning. At its distance of 1,600 light-years, we are gazing that far back into time. As you did in the "Meditating Upon a Star" exercise in Chapter 11, think about what was happening here on Earth over one and a half millennia ago, during the Dark Ages. What will the light that's just leaving the Trapezium tonight find when it arrives here 1,600 years from now? Will we have reached the stars by then? Or will humanity have proved itself to be ephemeral? We can only wonder. . . .

Is Our Sun a Double Star?

A persistent belief over the years is that the Sun itself is actually a double star! Is it possible that our Daytime Star has a dim red-dwarf companion perhaps a quarter or a half light-year away? It would be virtually impossible to see such a faint light submerged in the darkness of space directly with current telescopes, including the Hubble Space Telescope itself. But the gravitational effect on members of the solar system—especially the outer planets—might be detectable. Indeed, it was perturbations in the orbit of Uranus that resulted in the discovery of Neptune, and then discrepancies in its orbit that launched the search for Pluto.

There are still unexplained perturbations affecting members of the Sun's family, and some astronomers attribute them to the influence of a companion star. Others say they stem instead from the multitude of ice-ball worlds and comets that lie beyond the orbit of Pluto. Perhaps when the huge James Webb Space Telescope is eventually launched in a few years, we will be able to actually see the Sun's companion, if it's there.

Interestingly, if Jupiter had been several times as massive as it currently is, it would have become a star! Instead, it's often looked upon as a "failed star." But Arthur C. Clarke in his novel *2010: Odyssey Two* (sequel to *2001: A Space Odyssey*) imagined that Jupiter had acquired enough additional mass to turn it from a giant planet into a small newborn star, as astronauts watched it happen. Could a large rouge body someday enter the solar system and smash into Jupiter, causing this to occur?

In July of 1994 the astronomy world was electrified when huge Comet Shoemaker-Levy 9 unexpectedly broke into 21 separate pieces, each of which then spectacularly crashed into Jupiter's atmosphere! Their impacts were easily visible even in small telescopes.

When it comes to the universe, it truly seems that anything is possible! Shakespeare's immortal words from *Hamlet* come to mind: "There are more things in heaven and Earth, Horatio, / Than are dreamt of in your philosophy." And while on this topic, here's another of Clarke's famous dictums: "The only way to discover the limits of the possible is to go beyond them into the impossible." As we've seen, the cosmos certainly provides ample opportunities for doing just that!

We next transition from double- and multiple-star systems to larger assemblages—entire groups of suns all moving through space together as a family unit.

CHAPTER 14

STAR CLUSTERS

Celestial Families

As we saw in the last chapter, most of the stars in the sky are actually double or multiple systems consisting of as many as six members. But it doesn't stop there—a continuous cosmic hierarchy exists where dozens, hundreds, and even thousands of suns loosely congregate into *open clusters* (as opposed to highly compacted *globular clusters* containing upwards of a million stars, as described in the "Stellar Beehives" section later in this chapter).

These beautiful stellar communes are truly a sight to behold, in many cases even with the unaided eye! And their individual members are all bound together as a true family by gravity—not just chance aggregations of unrelated stars. The sky abounds with them, and here are just a few prominent specimens for your viewing pleasure.

The Pleiades

The most famous and striking open cluster in the sky is without question the Pleiades in the constellation Taurus, positioned northwest of Orion. Long a hallmark of the winter sky, it's perhaps better known by its popular name, the "Seven Sisters," from its half dozen or so brighter members.

The eye sees here a misty-looking group of stars in the shape of a small dipper, and in fact, it's often mistaken for the Little Dipper (Ursa Minor) itself, which is much larger and fainter. Binoculars transform it into a glittering stellar jewel box of sparkling blue-white diamonds! The Moon occasionally passes in front of the Pleiades (or *occults* it), with stars disappearing and re-appearing in a spectacular cosmic "hide-and-see" show. But the cluster itself lies far beyond our lovely satellite, at a distance of some 400 light-years (the Moon itself being less than 2 *light-seconds* away!).

It's intriguing that a number of cultures claim that their ancestors came from the Pleiades—most notably the Japanese, who have even named a car company after it (Subaru, whose emblem shows the primary stars in the cluster)! Where did they ever get that idea?

Well, let me share a personal experience with you that lends anecdotal support to this far-out concept. A number of years ago, I was speaking in Lower Manhattan at the New York Open Center. Following the formal presentation, I took everyone out onto the sidewalk to do some stargazing with my state-of-the-art Celestron telescope. (Yes—it's actually possible to stargaze from the heart of a major city like New York despite light pollution!) The final object I showed them that evening was the Pleiades.

A woman walking on the other side of the street stopped, looked our way, and then hesitantly crossed over to us. She inquired what we were doing, and I told her that we were looking at the stars. She asked if she could take a peek, since she'd never looked through a telescope before, and said she knew nothing about stars.

Of course I obliged without hesitation, as I'm very evangelistic (some would say obsessed!) about sharing the sky with others. She looked into the eyepiece and immediately burst into tears of joy, shouting, "That's my home!"

Now why would she ever think that?

The Hyades Cluster

Between Orion and the Pleiades is another beautiful open cluster obviously visible to the unaided eye known as the Hyades. In fact, a line drawn from Orion's three prominent belt stars upward in the sky points right at it—and then extended farther ends at the Pleiades. This group has a distinctive V shape and features as its crown jewel the bright topaz sun Aldebaran in its midst.

But appearances are not always what they seem, for this gem isn't actually part of the cluster itself. It lies 65 light-years away and is seen projected against the starry swarm, which is twice as remote, at a distance of 130 light-years. Nevertheless, the combined effect is indeed striking! Scanning the cluster with binoculars will reveal a number of neat double stars among its members. (Such glasses actually give a better view of large groups like this than do telescopes, which typically aren't able to encompass all of their stars at one time.) The Hyades is one of the very closest of such clans, which is why it appears so big and prominent in our sky.

The Beehive Cluster

In the dim constellation of Cancer, lying midway between Gemini and Leo is a faint fuzzy glow visible on clear, dark (moonless) nights in the spring. This marks the location of the Beehive Cluster, known since antiquity as the "Cloudy One," "Little Mist," and "Praesepe" (meaning "manger"). It was used by our ancestors (and still is today by some folks I know) as a weather forecaster. They regarded its visibility—or actually, lack thereof—as an indication of an approaching storm front.

Sharp-eyed observers using averted vision (see Chapter 4) will see individual points of light dimly shining within this glow. In binoculars, it fairly explodes into a lovely swarm of colorful stars! Using his primitive telescope, Galileo counted three dozen of them. But there are many more to be seen, especially in large glasses, where its appearance has been likened to that of a "diamond mine"! The Beehive glistens softly at us from across a distance of 590 light-years.

The Double Cluster

Just as individual stars form pairs, so do a number of star clusters themselves. And the most famous of these is the Double Cluster in the constellation Perseus, visible from the fall through winter months. It appears as a misty elongated glow to the unaided eye about mid-way between Perseus and Cassiopeia in the winter Milky Way. Binoculars are needed to see it as an actual double group of stars with their cores a full-Moon diameter apart in the sky. (A complete circle around the sky contains 360 degrees. The Moon as we see it has an angular size of about one-half of one of these degrees, and as such provides a useful gauge of the *apparent* size of various celestial objects.) And the Double Cluster is truly a magnificent sight in even the smallest of telescopes, where it appears as a dual starburst of multihued heavenly jewels!

Amazingly, the two clusters lie at the same distance from us (7,300 light-years) and are physically (gravitationally) connected. It's also believed that they are slowly orbiting each other, but the period must be on the order of *millions* of years. The Greek astronomer Hipparchus was the first to record this wonder, but it was surely seen by others much earlier under the pristine dark skies of antiquity.

The Alpha Persei Association

There are a number of very large scattered groups of stars in the sky called *stellar associations* that are not concentrated enough to be considered true open clusters. They are typically easily seen with the unaided eye and fascinating sights in binoculars—but not telescopes, due to their being too spread out.

And one of the most striking examples lies in Perseus not far from the Double Cluster itself. It's known as the Alpha Persei Association, after its brightest member, the 2nd-magnitude star Mirfak (Alpha Persei). This is the same star that was recommended as a magnitude reference for watching Algol "wink" in Chapter 12. The association itself consists of nearly a hundred stars scattered over five degrees (or ten full-Moon diameters) of sky, with "princely Mirfak enthroned in the midst of a truly royal council of stars," as one observer described it long ago.

Sweeping through this delightful group with binoculars, you'll find most of the stars here to be blue-white in hue, while Mirfak appears a lovely lilac to most eyes. Like the Double Cluster, this widespread stellar clan also lies in the winter Milky Way—but a dozen times closer to us, at a distance of 600 light-years.

Asterisms

Asterisms are distinctive stellar patterns lying within a constellation or, in some cases, one made up of those from two or more adjoining constellations. Undoubtedly the best known and most easily recognized of all asterisms is the Big Dipper (which, as I've previously mentioned, is *not* itself a constellation but rather part of Ursa Major). Some are so unusual and artificial looking that they seemingly couldn't possibly be real!

One of these is the famed "Coathanger" of the summer sky. To find it, we use another of the sky's asterisms—this one the huge Summer Triangle, discussed in Chapter 4, made up of the three bright, blue-white stars Vega, Deneb, and Altair. The Coathanger lies about one-third of the way along a line from Altair to Vega, appearing as a bright patch in the Milky Way to the unaided eye on a dark, moonless night.

Much smaller and fainter than the Big Dipper itself, this amazing object appears as an upside-down starry coat hanger! It consists of six stars in a straight line and a curved hook at the center made up of four more. Also known as Brocchi's Cluster, after its discoverer, it's a delightful surprise to come across it while sweeping its location with binoculars. And sharp-eyed observers may also make out its unusual shape even without optical aid. However, despite appearances, this object is not a true cluster of related stars but rather a chance alignment of them lying at different distances from us.

An evening of leisurely stargazing exploring the sky with binoculars will turn up many other unusual-looking asterisms. But none can match the remarkable appearance of the Coathanger itself. Here's another one for your "must-see" list of celestial treasures!

Stellar Beehives

We now turn our attention to ball-shaped swarms of stars known as *globular clusters,* containing hundreds of thousands—up to as many as a million—individual suns! (Often referred to as *beehives* from their appearance, they are not to be confused with the Beehive Cluster itself, described previously.) Unlike open clusters, which are scattered all along the plane of our Milky Way Galaxy, globulars reside in a vast spherical halo surrounding the galactic nucleus centered in the direction of the summer constellation Sagittarius. As a result, these stellar beehives are mainly visible during the summer months, while open clusters can be seen throughout much of the year.

Viewing a globular cluster in a large telescope is an experience never to be forgotten, and another compelling reason for attending an observatory open house or astronomy-club star party. Imagine a hundred thousand glittering stars suspended against a black velvet background staring you right in the eye! The best way I can describe it is like driving in a snowy blizzard at night, with the "snowflakes" being stars frozen in time! It leaves the onlooker all but speechless and in reverent awe. And while at least a small telescope is needed to appreciate their grandeur, many can be seen with binoculars and even a few with the unaided eye. Here are two noted examples of the latter—one for Northern Hemisphere stargazers and the other primarily for Southern Hemisphere viewers.

The Hercules Cluster

Named after the summer constellation in which it resides, the Hercules Cluster appears as a fuzzy-looking 6th-magnitude star on the western (right) side of the central "Keystone" of this legendary hero. Remembering again that we must "see" with the mind as well as sight, within that dim blob are several hundred thousand suns, all orbiting its center like a swarm of bees. At its core, the sky is filled with countless numbers of stars appearing as bright as Venus when at its greatest brilliancy! There are so many, in fact, that there is no real night there at all.

This scene reminds me of Isaac Asimov's classic science-fiction short story "Nightfall." It's based on this famous line from Emerson: "If the stars should appear one night in a thousand years, how would men believe and adore; and preserve for many generations the remembrance of the city of God which had been shown!" The story is about a civilization living on a planet in a multiple-star system having so many suns in the sky that it never gets dark—except once in a thousand years. When it finally does, the sky is filled with stars, for their system lies on the edge of a huge globular cluster!

I well remember the first time I saw this magnificent star ball from my backyard observatory using a fairly large telescope. It was 3 A.M. and I screamed out loud: "Oh my God! Look at that! How can anybody possibly be sleeping when this is hanging right over their heads?" Suddenly, neighbors' bedroom windows began slamming shut (it was summer), with comments to the effect of "Well, we're not sleeping *now!*"

This is a marvelous object to meditate upon, even if only appearing as a fuzzy star in your binoculars.

Meditative Moment

As you gaze upon the Hercules Cluster, realize that the light entering your eyes tonight left there 24,000 years ago, when cave dwellers were still hunting mastodon, and is just now arriving. (The cluster is 24,000 light-years away.) And then think about an amazing calculation that has been performed concerning the odds of any two of the stars ever colliding with each other, even in the crowded center of that remote stellar beehive. It's statistically akin to someone catching a fly in the United States, another person doing so in Australia, and then both releasing their flies simultaneously. The chance that they will ever run into each other— flying all around the Earth—is the same as two stars ever colliding! Talk about divine order in the universe!

Omega Centauri

Should you live in the Southern Hemisphere—or along the southern portion of the United States—you can view a globular cluster that's far brighter, larger, and more spectacular than the one in Hercules. It lies in the spring constellation Centaurus, the Centaur, located 40 degrees due south of Spica. (This is the bright star at the end of the arc that begins in the Big Dipper's handle, as discussed in Chapter 4.) It is so prominent that it was assigned a Greek letter by early star mappers and thus is known as Omega Centauri. It looks like a fuzzy 4th-magnitude star to the eye. Even binoculars will show it to be a ball of stars, while the telescopic view is truly beyond the ability of words to adequately describe.

This colossal stellar beehive contains well over a *million* suns! And to think as we watch that it's serenely orbiting the center of our galaxy. Oh, what a superb example of heavenly glory! We view this marvel of the night from across a distance of some 17,000 light-years. I've long desired to astral-travel to the center of one of these glorious spheres, if only for just a few seconds. It hasn't happened yet, but anytime I view a globular cluster, the thought is always on my mind. Perhaps someday I'll get there!

You might be wondering just where all the various kinds of stars we've been discussing came from. Well—just like you and me—they were *born!* And our next chapter explores how and where.

CHAPTER 15

THE NEBULAE

Star Nurseries

Hidden deep within vast clouds of hydrogen gas are pockets of ice and dust around which the gas itself begins to condense, forming spinning *protostars*—baby stars in the making within a cosmic womb or "nursery." These stellar infants glow ever hotter and spin faster and faster as they become more compressed. At some critical point, the temperature and pressure become great enough for thermonuclear reactions to begin and a star is born! And as I mentioned at the beginning of Chapter 12, while it takes millions of years for this birthing process to happen, the initiation of the nuclear reactions themselves occurs within just *three minutes!*

It's one of the sacred privileges of being a professional astronomer today to be able to watch the birth of new worlds right before one's eyes! This is made possible by instruments like the Hubble Space Telescope, combined with the amazing electro-optical imaging technology that has all but replaced conventional film photography.

But you don't need the Hubble to take part in this cosmic drama. At least three star nurseries can be seen by stargazers with the unaided eye (two of them from the Southern Hemisphere) and several others using binoculars. And while they may not look like much more than a fuzzy little blob without using a telescope, you *are* seeing the birthplaces of new stars and planets! Especially in viewing "faint fuzzies," like nebulae (and galaxies—to be covered in the next chapter), seeing with your mind as well as sight is imperative!

Nebulae themselves are divided into two main types: bright *diffuse nebulae* (stellar birthplaces) and *planetary nebulae* (stellar crypts, discussed later in the chapter). There are also *dark nebulae*, which are obscuring clouds of dust and gas that create apparent "holes" in the sky and which will be discussed in the next chapter, on the Milky Way.

What follows are a few of the most majestic and best-known nebulae, starting with the diffuse variety.

The Orion Nebula

Many consider this beautiful star nursery in the constellation Orion to be the finest of all deep-space wonders. And with good reason. It is overpowering as seen in large telescopes and absolutely exquisite in photographs. In smaller glasses, we see an emerald-green, fan-shaped cloud with the diamond-like Trapezium, described in Chapter 13, embedded within it.

Binoculars will show some of this glory, with the unresolved foursome appearing as one bright star at the heart of the nebulosity. And yes, you *can* see the Orion Nebula with the unaided eye! It's the middle "star" in Orion's sword, just under his three prominent belt stars. Look carefully and you'll notice that it definitely is fuzzy and not at all starlike. Having already spawned the Trapezium and many fainter stars surrounding it, this "star factory" is slowly turning its nebulous substance into an entire cluster of suns!

Many pages could be filled with the superlatives uttered by stargazers over the centuries upon seeing this spectacle of the winter sky, but here are a few that have appeared in observing logs: "Thrilling beyond words!" "Overpowering sublimity!" "Incomparable splendor!" "Aesthetic shock!" I've personally experienced all of these emotions, and more, in my many years of contemplating the Orion Nebula.

And while I'd be hard-pressed to ever explain it, looking at this wonder of the night—at creation unfolding right before my eyes—is a spiritual experience for me. As with the sight of other celestial marvels, the words *Praise God* silently and spontaneously form on my lips. The light from this beautiful nursery has traveled 1,600 years to reach us so it can "wow" you and me with its unearthly beauty.

The Tarantula Nebula

Our Milky Way has two companion galaxies known as the Magellanic Clouds. Both objects lie near the south pole of the sky and are only visible from the Southern Hemisphere. (Being "circumpolar," they can be seen year-round, depending on your actual latitude.) Within the larger of the two is a brilliant nebulous mass on its eastern (left) edge called the Tarantula Nebula due to the many "legs" spreading out from its core. It's readily visible to the unaided eye despite being 170,000 light-years from us.

The fact that it can be seen without optical aid at such a great distance indicates that it's intrinsically extremely bright. Indeed, if the Tarantula were as close to us as the Orion Nebula, it would span 70 degrees (140 full-Moon diameters) of sky and likely cast shadows! This glorious cloud defies description in binoculars and small telescopes, and is a "must-see" not only for those living south of the equator but also for anyone traveling there.

The Eta Carinae Nebula

Located in the constellation Carina is another big, bright star nursery visible from the Southern Hemisphere (and also from the Florida Keys when at its highest in the sky during northern spring). It's named after the star Eta Carinae, at the heart of the nebulosity. This is the massive, erratic sun mentioned in Chapter 12, which a number of astronomers believe is ready to go supernova!

Obvious at a glance to the naked eye, the Eta Carinae Nebula is truly a fascinating sight in binoculars. Some consider it the finest object of its class in the entire sky, even surpassing the magnificent Orion Nebula itself! Measuring two degrees (four full-Moon diameters) in size, its appearance in the telescope has been described as "blossoming forth like a huge ghostly orchid." Embedded within the nebulosity are many newborn stars.

Should this wonder be visible from where you live, be sure to keep an eye on Eta itself. Distance estimates range between 7,000 and 10,000 light-years from us.

This means that it may have already gone supernova long ago, and the light from that outburst is on its way to us. *And it could arrive at any time!*

The Lagoon Nebula

Here's another famous diffuse nebula visible from the Northern Hemisphere that's bright enough that it should be a naked-eye object. But it's suspended against the backdrop of a very rich region of the Milky Way in the summer constellation Sagittarius, making it a challenge to pick out. However, the view in binoculars is another story.

Sagittarius is marked by the striking "Teapot" asterism (it really does look like a giant teapot in the sky!). Scanning northward of its "spout" with binoculars will show a small nebulous cloud. Look carefully, and you will see that it's divided in two by a dark obscuring lane, giving rise to this nebula's name. You'll also see a knot of stars just to its east (left), which is a cluster apparently spawned by the nebula itself. This star nursery lies 5,000 light-years from us. Sweeping above the Lagoon will reveal many other nebulous-looking objects and star clusters in this amazingly rich region of the heavens, including the Trifid Nebula and the graceful Swan Nebula (both of which require a telescope in order to see why they were given their names).

Stellar Crypts

The *planetary nebulae,* so named because some of them resemble the planets Uranus and Neptune as seen in a telescope, are the second major type of nebulosity. They are the rings and spheres of gas being ejected out into space from their central suns. Unlike the diffuse nebulae that mark the beginning of stars' lives, these lovely objects signal their death throes. (But as mentioned in Chapter 12, this is not a cause for sadness. For, from the "ashes" of the old stars the new ones are born, in an ongoing cosmic cycle. And the hearts of the dying stars continue to live on in the form of white dwarfs, neutron stars, and black holes!)

Of the many wondrous forms these aged nebulosities assume (including many that look like flowers and seashells), the most significant to me spiritually are the ones shaped like butterflies—which is fitting, given these are widely recognized symbols of transformation and rebirth! Most of the planetaries are small in apparent size and require a telescope to appreciate their amazing diversity and exquisite beauty. But a number of the larger ones are visible in binoculars.

The mentor for more than 50 years of all who love observing "deep-sky wonders" was the late Walter Scott Houston, who penned a column in *Sky & Telescope* from 1946 to 1993. He once described planetary nebulae as "ephemeral spheres that shine in pale hues of blue and green and float amid the golden and pearly star currents of our Galaxy . . . on the foam of the Milky Way like the balloons of our childhood dreams." (Houston was also famous for saying "But let's forget the astrophysics and simply enjoy the spectacle" of a starry night!)

The Helix/Eye of God/Sunflower Nebula

The biggest planetary nebula in the sky is the one whose image from the Hubble Space Telescope graces the front cover of this book. To emphasize the spirituality that lies at the heart of this celestial guide (and the universe itself!), I selected it since it's widely referred to popularly as the "Eye of God."

It's also the closest nebula of its type to us, at 450 light-years, most others being thousands of light-years distant. This accounts for its huge size as planetaries go, which is half that of the Moon's apparent diameter in the sky. This multi-named wonder lies in the fall constellation Aquarius, in a blank-looking area northwest of the bright, blue-white star Fomalhaut (itself marking the constellation Piscis Austrinus, the Southern Fish). Sweep this spot on a dark, transparent night with the Moon absent using binoculars, and look for a round, dim, hazy patch of grayish light. Using larger glasses, you may be able to glimpse the "iris" in this celestial eyeball with averted vision.

The Ring Nebula

This object is the iconic image of a planetary nebula and the most famous member of its class in the entire sky (although it could be argued by some that it shares this distinction with the Dumbbell Nebula, described next). It's another celestial smoke ring or doughnut—this one located in the summer constellation Lyra, just south of blue-white Vega. It lies midway between the stars Beta and Gamma Lyrae, making it a snap to find its location. But actually seeing it in binoculars takes some concentration. It appears as a tiny, fuzzy-looking dim spot of light. In even a small telescope, its central hole becomes visible and it looks for all the world like an oval-shaped ring of blown smoke floating amid the stars! In large backyard telescopes or observatory instruments, it's truly an amazing sight never to be forgotten.

The Ring is 2,300 light-years from us—about a hundred times as far away as Vega itself! And while it looks tiny in binoculars, think about this: that spot of light you're seeing is *500 times the size of our entire solar system!*

The Dumbbell Nebula

This puffy cloud resides in the dim summer constellation Vulpecula, just beneath Cygnus. Sweep southeast of the beautiful double star Albireo with binoculars, and you'll find it looking like a small hazy, rectangular smudge. Large glasses and small telescopes reveal its hourglass shape, which led to its popular name.

Meditative Moment

The Dumbbell Nebula appears like a puffy heavenly pillow serenely floating among the stars of the Milky Way. Viewing it through binoculars (and especially with a telescope) may well put you into a sleepy dream state, as it does for me. Perhaps it's the pillow image that's responsible! Realize that the ethereal light you see from it tonight is the way it looked 1,200 years ago when leaving there and that it surely has changed in appearance over those many centuries. As is the case for all such celestial wonders, the photons emanating from it come on and on across space and time in a never-ending stream while you continue to gaze upon it. May they help you sleep peacefully tonight!

The Crab Nebula

In Chapter 12, I talked about the celebrated supernova seen by Chinese astronomers in A.D. 1054 that gave birth to this object. Although originally thought to be a planetary nebula, the Crab is actually classified today as a *supernova remnant*—one of only a handful of such objects found in the heavens. It's located in the winter constellation Taurus, very close to the star Zeta Tauri. Despite its relative faintness, it's plotted on most star maps due to its fame (and also its cosmic significance).

The nebulosity's serrated outline and crablike filaments seen on photographs (giving rise to its name) are expanding outward in all directions at a rate of more than *two million miles per hour!* Observatory images clearly show the Crab growing in size from this expansion. In binoculars it appears as only a faint elongated smudge of light. But, oh, think about what that smudge represents!

Meditative Moment

The faint glow emanating from the Crab Nebula is the remains of a supermassive giant sun! And consider this as well: At its distance of more than 6,000 light-years, the supernova explosion itself <u>actually happened over 60 centuries before Chinese astronomers saw it in the sky!</u> At that time, their Neolithic forebears would have only recently begun to cultivate crops and craft pottery. The amount of time it took for the light from this catastrophic event to reach Planet Earth, moving at a speed of 186,000 miles per second, would have spanned the emergence of civilization, including the rise and fall of a dozen Chinese dynasties. How utterly amazing!

Another fascinating aspect of the Crab Nebula is the rapidly spinning neutron star at its heart. As it spins *30 times a second,* it sends out optical and radio pulses in our direction like some cosmic lighthouse. Thus, it's also classified as a *pulsar.* (All neutron stars are, in fact, likely to be pulsars. But their beams in most cases are not aimed in our direction, so they don't appear to "pulse.")

When first discovered, pulsars set astronomers' hearts racing, for it was actually thought that they were some kind of interstellar beacon directing space-faring "traffic" across our galaxy! (Some of the signals were even labeled *LGM,* for "Little Green Men.") Unfortunately, the excitement didn't last long, as the real source of the "signals" was soon traced to spinning neutron stars themselves. But there are those of us who still believe that such beacons could—and indeed, *should*—exist out there among the stars!

In fact, there are virtually an unlimited number of places for extraterrestrial navigation beacons to be located within the vastness of our home galaxy, which we examine next.

CHAPTER 16

THE MILKY WAY

Our Home Galaxy

One of the most magnificent sights in all of nature surely has to be the awesome sweep of the Milky Way encircling the night sky, for this is our home! Some 100,000 light-years across, it's about 15,000 light-years thick at its central hub and tapers off to as little as 5,000 light-years at its very edge.

We reside about two-thirds of the way out from the center, which is located in the direction of the constellation Sagittarius. On summer nights we're looking into its thickest and richest regions, while in winter we're facing the opposite direction and seeing its thin outer portions—with the result that our galaxy is much less obvious and striking during that season. (In spring and fall, the Milky Way lies along the horizon, and we look out at right angles to its long dimension into intergalactic space to the realm of the other galaxies themselves.)

This giant pinwheel contains perhaps as many as *500 billion stars* and countless planets! At our distance from its nucleus, it takes 220 million years for the Sun and its planets to orbit the galaxy once! In *Paradise Lost*, John Milton poetically described the glorious Milky Way to be "A broad and ample road, whose dust is gold, / And pavement stars." And so it appears.

The Great White Way

New York City's famed Great White Way isn't the only thoroughfare to be so named. There's a far vaster one visible from anywhere on the planet, and it's in the sky! I'm referring, of course, to the grand thoroughfare of our home galaxy. Summer and fall evenings are the best times to see and experience its magnificence. And to do so, you need nothing more than just your eyes, and a dark (moonless), clear night. The exercise on the facing page contains my suggestions on how to enjoy this awesome wonder.

The Scutum Star Cloud

Between Aquila and Sagittarius lies the little constellation Scutum, the Shield. Just 9 degrees by 12 degrees in size, it's totally filled with an amazingly rich star cloud referred to as the "Gem of the Milky Way" and also as "Downtown Milky Way"! Obvious to the unaided eye, it is glorious beyond description in binoculars (and also in small telescopes having a very low-power, wide field of view). The stars of our galaxy are perhaps more tightly packed together here than in any other part of the Milky Way. Many stargazers consider this the sky's largest and finest deep-space wonder. I defy anyone to see it, as I have, in 10×50mm binoculars or a 15×75mm spotting scope and not let out a gasp of astonished delight!

EXERCISE:
Viewing the Milky Way

Reclining in a lawn chair is the most relaxing and enjoyable way to explore the Milky Way as it arches high overhead. Avoid sources of bright illumination such as porch and street lights, and give your eyes a chance to fully adjust to the night by remaining in darkness for 10 to 15 minutes. Take this time to identify the starry outlines of the brighter constellations using the star maps in *Sky & Telescope* or *Astronomy* (and a red light to maintain your dark adaptation while doing so) or a smartphone/tablet app. Note how the pale radiance of the Milky Way shown on these maps stretches from the northeastern horizon all the way across the sky to the southwestern one, passing nearly overhead at these seasons of the year.

Now compare this to the real sky—especially where its rich star stream courses through the constellations Cygnus, Aquila, Scutum, and Scorpius, and, most majestically, in the direction of the galaxy's center located just off the "Teapot" asterism in Sagittarius. There, its big billowy star clouds are so intense that many actually mistake them for rain clouds forming! (In keeping with the idea of a teapot, the Milky Way looks like steam coming from its spout!)

Taking your exploration a step further, use binoculars to sweep along the entire course of the galaxy from horizon to horizon. It will suddenly come alive with beautiful, multihued suns, glittering star clusters, fascinating asterisms, and misty-looking nebulosities. You will then sense as never before the awesome majesty of our Milky Way Galaxy in all its glory! Seeing it this way may well be beauty in its purest form.

Its only "competitor" for sheer visual Milky Way shock is the Small Sagittarius Star Cloud, which is a particularly rich part of that constellation's main cloud. It's these two grand areas of our galaxy that have inspired and thrilled countless star lovers over the centuries who have simply taken the time to retreat under the pale mystical radiance and looked up in contemplative silence.

In Chapter 3, I talked about out-of-body experiences and astral travel to the stars. And as promised, I want to share a method by which you may possibly experience this for yourself using the Milky Way. While this amazing effect can be seen just staring at it without optical aid, I've found that binoculars (especially wide-angle ones) enhance the chance of it occurring.

EXERCISE:
Seeing Our Galaxy in 3-D

- Venturing outdoors on a dark (moonless), clear night, begin by getting comfortably seated—or recline on a lawn chair.

- Allow time for your eyes to get dark-adapted. As much as possible, avoid distractions such as passing cars, neighbors talking, or television screens flashing through the windows of surrounding houses.

- Next, look at the Milky Way's big billowy star clouds—especially where it passes through Cygnus, Scutum, and Sagittarius. Notice that the brighter stars in these clouds appear to be closer to you than the fainter ones—*that you are actually seeing layer upon layer of stars at different distances from you.*

- As you allow the eye-brain combination to make this connection, the Milky Way *may suddenly jump right out of the sky at you* as the huge starry pinwheel it actually is! It's during this striking illusion of depth perception that you may find yourself for a few brief moments "out there" among the lights in the sky. Even if this doesn't happen to you, seeing the Milky Way as a vast three-dimensional structure certainly makes this exercise worth doing. (And, of course, be sure to try again on another night!)

The Search for Extraterrestrial Life

Ever since radio astronomer Frank Drake's historic 1960 "Project Ozma," in which he attempted to detect artificial radio signals from two nearby Sun-like stars beamed to us by an advanced civilization, an intensive search of the skies for such beings has been under way at radio-astronomy observatories throughout the world. According to the SETI Institute in California, supposedly no definite artificial radio signals have been detected to date. (There are those both within the astronomical community and outside of it who doubt this.)

And the search today doesn't involve only radio telescopes but optical ones as well, which are looking for pulsed laser signals from the stars. Due to the vast distances of the other galaxies from us, extraterrestrial contact will likely come from somewhere within our own Milky Way. And there are surely enough worlds out there for this to happen.

Meditative Moment

Recall that there are more stars within reach of our largest telescopes today than all the grains of sand on the entire Earth, and when you look at the Milky Way's vast star clouds, consider how absolutely absurd it would be to think that we are the only intelligent beings in creation. But as mentioned earlier in this book, astronomers and exobiologists are now convinced that the galaxy, and indeed, the entire universe, is thriving with life—that we are, in fact, living in a bio-cosmos! This makes viewing the stars, and the Milky Way in particular, so very exciting: just think that there are other beings out there looking back at us and wondering, as we do, if they are alone.

The Emissaries Are Coming!

In Arthur C. Clarke's classic science-fiction short story "The Sentinel" (the basis for his later best-selling novel *2001: A Space Odyssey* and the blockbuster movie directed by Stanley Kubrick), astronauts accidentally trigger a beacon left on the Moon by an advanced race from the stars. Having done so, the narrator delivers this provocative and thrilling line: "I can never look now at the Milky Way without wondering from which of those banked clouds of stars the emissaries are coming." And I often have the same thought whenever I'm stargazing.

Of course, we here on Earth have long been beaming radio and television "messages" unintentionally to the stars as our broadcasts leak out into space. (I shudder to think what the aliens must wonder about our civilization given the sad state of TV programming today!) But there has been at least one intentional powerful broadcast beamed to the stars by astronomers.

The "Arecibo Interstellar Message" (as it is known) was sent using the colossal 1,000-foot-diameter radio telescope at the Arecibo Observatory in Puerto Rico on November 16, 1974. The brainchild of Carl Sagan and Frank Drake, it was beamed to the Hercules Star Cluster, described in Chapter 14. The transmission contained a vast amount of coded information about us, our star, and our planet.

At the star cluster's distance of 24,000 light-years, the radio waves would require 48,000 years for any reply to make the round-trip traveling at the speed of light. (That is, unless the recipients in this stellar beehive have found a shortcut through space and time for sending messages—which is not so unlikely, given that its stars are at least twice the age of our own Sun and its planets, and they would have had many more years in which to develop this technology.) The reason for selecting a globular cluster instead of targeting just a single star was that the signal would encompass more than 100,000 suns in one sweep and immensely increase the likelihood of it being received by "someone" there.

The Encyclopaedia Galactica

The 12th episode of Carl Sagan's widely acclaimed, Emmy-winning PBS television series *Cosmos* is titled "Encyclopaedia Galactica." It concerns the thrilling likelihood (some would say "certainty") that our Milky Way Galaxy is not only teeming with intelligent life but that these other civilizations are communicating with each other and sharing knowledge. Furthermore, it speculates that there is a repository of information collected from all over the galaxy throughout the ages, supplied by its many inhabitants. And this amazing treasure trove is available to any civilization advanced enough to tap into it! Can you possibly even imagine that?

The communication itself linking these societies is assumed to be by radio or optical means. (The Arecibo radio telescope is capable of communicating with a similar-sized dish anywhere in the Milky Way Galaxy! What's more, even at our present level of technology, this instrument could transmit the entire contents of the *Encyclopaedia Britannica* in just a matter of days!) But there may be other wildly sophisticated methods being used, like neutrino modulation, or ones we haven't yet discovered. As suggested in Chapter 3, it may even be that truly advanced beings aren't using any technical means at all—they may be communicating instantly, telepathically!

> ## Meditative Moment
>
> *I love to imagine when looking up at the Milky Way at night what these other civilizations are saying to each other about things like their science or religion or philosophy or the arts. Have they solved the big questions of existence yet that so haunt us? We can only wonder—and hope.*

Angels as ETs?

Scripture, classic literature, and folklore are filled with references to angelic beings. Countless books have been written about angels and their interaction with humans. To me, though, the two most fascinating accounts come from space:

1. One is the account of the Russian cosmonauts who were dying from lack of oxygen due to a leak in the pressurization system of their Mir spacecraft as it orbited the Earth. Suddenly, they saw several angels hovering outside their window—apparently smiling and waving at them! This has been attributed to hallucination resulting from oxygen deprivation in the brain. But miraculously (and unexplainably), the spacecraft repressurized itself and they were saved. The cosmonauts themselves are convinced that they saw the real thing.

2. The other account involves the blue auras that appeared around both moonwalkers on the second Moon landing, Apollo 12. There's no doubt that these glows were real and not the result of the cameras that captured

them or the film processing. Both astronauts are on record as saying that those glows *were their guardian angels!*

Whatever actually happened to those men in orbit, and on the surface of the Moon, there appears to be little doubt that "someone" was protecting them. In discussing extraterrestrial beings, could it be that at least some of them belong to the angelic realm? It seems more than likely to me!

The Dark Side of the Milky Way

In addition to the visible stars and nebulae making up the Milky Way, there are areas of dark material obscuring what lies beyond them and which were originally thought to be actual holes in the sky! Some of these are small opaque spheres, called *Bok Globules,* requiring a telescope to be seen. They represent protostars in the process of condensing out of the interstellar medium.

Other areas are much larger and quite obvious to the unaided eye, two of which are the famous *Coal Sacks* of the sky. One is located next to the well-known Southern Cross asterism and is visible only from the Southern Hemisphere. The other lies in Cygnus's Northern Cross asterism and is prominently visible in the summer and fall sky. (Isn't it an interesting coincidence that both of these dark abysses are associated with heavenly crosses?) To see the Northern Cross one, look just south of the constellation's bright, blue-white luminary Deneb on a dark, moonless night. It's an obvious "hole" or break in the star clouds. Scanning it with binoculars is a fascinating experience, and they will also show a number of stars actually scattered about within it.

The most obvious dark nebulae in the Milky Way are the *Great Dark Rifts* that seemingly split it apart in places. And the most dramatic of these also happens to lie in Cygnus. Beginning with the Coal Sack itself, the Cygnus rift meanders southward through that constellation and continues all the way through neighboring Aquila and into Ophiuchus, the Serpent Bearer.

Over a century ago, the great astronomer Edward Emerson Barnard produced the first photographic atlas of the Milky Way, which showed its amazing richness and diversity—along with hundreds of dark nebulae of all sizes and shapes. (Among the fanciful names given to some of them are the Snake Nebula, the Pipe Nebula, and the S Nebula.) A fascinating aspect of using binoculars (especially wide-angle ones, which typically can take in 12 or more full-Moon diameters of sky) to view these objects is that *many of them appear to be suspended against the starry background* in striking relief!

Our home galaxy is indeed an amazing place. Realize that all of the wonders that we've explored together since setting out on our "cosmic journey" have been within the confines of our own Milky Way. But just as in the case of the solar system, it's only a "drop in the ocean" of intergalactic space. We now venture ever further outward, into the true "great beyond"—to the vast realm of the other galaxies!

CHAPTER 17

GALAXIES & QUASARS

Island Universes

Although the nebulous patches of light we now call *galaxies* had been known for centuries, it was only in the 1930s that astronomers had proof that they were not part of, and inside, the Milky Way but far beyond it in the depths of intergalactic space. They looked different from the diffuse and planetary nebulae—many of them having a spiral form that the other nebulae didn't, and they all had a kind of "remote" appearance to them.

Then Edwin Hubble (for whom the Hubble Space Telescope is named), using the 100-inch reflector at the Mount Wilson Observatory, finally resolved some of them into their individual stars, proving at last that they are indeed other galaxies—or *island universes,* as they were subsequently called—like our own Milky Way. The sheer number of these "star cities in the night" visible in our largest telescopes today is staggering. It's estimated to be on the order of *100 billion!* And each of these in turn may contain as many as a *trillion* individual stars!

The Andromeda Galaxy

Despite their vast distances from us (measured in *millions* of light-years), there are a surprising number of galaxies visible to the unaided eye for your viewing pleasure and contemplation. Add binoculars and the number reaches the hundreds, while even a small telescope will literally show *thousands* of them! It's always intrigued me that Universal Intelligence has made it possible to personally see every major unit of creation in the heavens with just our eyes alone. I personally don't think that is just a coincidence.

The grandest and most magnificent galaxy in the sky is, of course, our own Milky Way. Next comes the iconic Andromeda Galaxy, visible during the fall and winter months in the constellation Andromeda. Despite its distance of 2.4 million light-years, it's obvious to the unaided eye on a dark, clear moonless night. It was even recognized by ancient stargazers, who referred to it as the "Little Cloud." This beautiful spiral is nearly a clone of our own galaxy and is easily found, thanks to the Great Square of Pegasus asterism described in Chapter 4. Following an imaginary line from the bottom right corner star of the Square (actually a rectangle) to its upper left corner one (a star Pegasus shares with neighboring Andromeda) prolonged its own distance brings you to 2nd-magnitude Beta Andromedae. The "Great Spiral of Andromeda" (as it's often called) lies just a short distance to the upper right (northwest) of that star. To the unaided eye, it appears as a misty oval smudge of light that's clearly non-stellar in appearance.

Switching now to binoculars: Sweeping slowly back and forth across its bright core, combined with the use of averted vision, will show this object to be several times the apparent size of the full Moon. The faint outer halo you see is composed of countless numbers of unresolved stars in its disk and spiral arms.

And just as our galaxy has two companions (the Large and Small Magellanic Clouds, discussed in Chapter 15 under the "Tarantula Nebula" heading), so too does our neighbor. One looks like a fuzzy star just southeast of its main glow and the other a dim oval to the northwest of it. Larger glasses or a small telescope may be required to make them out, depending on just how clear the night is and also on how well you've trained your eye to see such "faint fuzzies." Telescopes will also reveal a tiny, starlike nucleus, and subtle dark areas in the main glow, which are actually dust lanes between the spiral arms themselves.

An interesting exercise is to compare observatory photographs of the Andromeda Galaxy to what you see in binoculars and telescopes. Here, truly, is an object of increasing interest and wonder the longer you gaze at it.

Meditative Moment

Reporter Sharon Renzulli, after interviewing a number of stargazers, stated: "Some amateur astronomers, it is said, experience the 'rapture of the depths' when observing the Andromeda Galaxy." I'm definitely one of them! And many other stargazers I know as well—some of whom often stare at this remote wonder for hours at a time, as if in a trance. Take a look for yourself and you'll see why! Just think: it took the light entering your eyes tonight 24,000 centuries to reach you—and yet, it's one of the closest galaxies to us!

The Whirlpool Galaxy

The Andromeda Galaxy serenely sails the ocean of intergalactic space tipped to our line of sight by some 15 degrees. Other galaxies we see face-on and yet others edge-on. In this section and the next one, I'll present an example of each. Unfortunately, neither is visible to the unaided eye, but they *can* be glimpsed in binoculars. In telescopes, they're quite striking. In both cases, use Hubble Space Telescope images of them from **www.hubble site.org** to see what those faint blobs of light *really* look like! (Here, once again, is the importance of seeing with your mind as well as sight.)

As its name suggests, the Whirlpool Galaxy has a majestic system of graceful spiral arms spreading outward from its nucleus, which we view looking right down on top of them. You'll find it off the star at the end of the Big Dipper's handle (Eta Ursae Majoris), where it forms an equilateral triangle with it and a fainter star (24 Ursae Majoris). Telescopes (and photos) show this object as double, for it has a small companion galaxy seemingly being flung off of one of the spiral arms. Some stargazers have likened the Whirlpool's appearance to an eternal celestial question mark. It graces our spring and summer skies from across a distance of more than 30 million light-years.

The Sombrero Galaxy

Spring is really "galaxy time," as that's when we look out of the Milky Way at right angles to the galactic plane into deep space. And here's one of the brightest and best of these island universes. Oriented nearly edge-on to our view, the Sombrero Galaxy has a prominent dark equatorial band (the "hat brim") and bulbous center, lending it its popular name. (Many have also likened its appearance to the classic image of a flying saucer!)

It lurks in the constellation Virgo precisely at the corner of a right triangle formed by the stars Spica and Porrima (Gamma Virginis, itself a famous close binary star for telescopes). This makes finding its position in the sky a breeze—but actually seeing it in binoculars requires careful attention. You're looking for a small, nebulous, egg-shaped blob.

Meditative Moment

Once you find the Sombrero, think about this: You are looking at one of the largest and richest galaxies known. It has over 2,000 globular clusters in its halo alone (the Milky Way has a few hundred), each of which contains up to a million suns! The total number of stars in that little blob must be close to a trillion! Distance estimates for this monster galaxy are very divergent, but 50 million light-years is the value typically quoted. And yet you can see the Sombrero across that immense gulf of space from your own backyard or balcony in a basic pair of binoculars on a dark night. Now that's truly amazing!

The Pinwheel/Triangulum Galaxy

Just southeast of the Andromeda Galaxy in the neighboring constellation of Triangulum, the Triangle, is another big spiral that can just be glimpsed with the unaided eye under excellent sky conditions in the fall and winter. It lies roughly the same distance southeast of the star Beta Andromedae as the Andromeda Galaxy is northwest of it. It is really big and bright as galaxies go. Its "integrated" or total magnitude is above the naked-eye limit for dark skies. But its light is spread out over an area nearly the size of the full Moon, resulting in a very low "surface brightness."

Binoculars make spotting it much easier. However, it's so big that it's possible to pass right over it in a telescope and not realize you're seeing it! It's a beauty in photos, and you'll see why it's called the Pinwheel (a name it shares with two other galaxies in different parts of the sky). This is the closest of the spiral galaxies after Andromeda, at a distance of 3.6 million light-years.

Realm of the Galaxies

So far, we've talked about isolated galaxies, a couple of which have companions. But galaxies are a gregarious lot, and they love to congregate in groups and clusters, just as stars themselves do. The Milky Way, together with the Andromeda Galaxy and the Pinwheel/Triangulum Galaxy, is the largest and brightest of several dozen star cities that form the *Local Group.* This small cluster, in turn, is part of the enormous *Coma-Virgo Cluster,* which contains some 10,000 galaxies! It's named for the two spring constellations Coma Berenices and Virgo over which this vast horde of island universes is spread. None of the individual members of this amazing "Realm of the Galaxies," as it's popularly called (an older alternative title is "Realm of the Nebulae"), are visible to the unaided eye. However, dozens of ghostly looking dim

glows can be glimpsed sweeping this area with binoculars on a dark night (and more than a thousand in backyard telescopes).

The densest part of this cloud lies between the stars
Denebola (Beta Leonis) in the constellation Leo to the
west and Vindemiatrix (Epsilon Virginis) in the constellation Virgo to the east. Even without optical aid, I love
to stare at this dark expanse of sky and think about all
that lurks out there in the great beyond.

> ### Meditative Moment
>
> *Our Local Group is positioned on the outer edge of the
> main swarm of the Coma-Virgo cluster, whose core lies 70
> million light-years from our Milky Way. We can only wonder
> what colossal forces came together to create this magnifi-
> cent assemblage. Was it, as many scientists and nonscien-
> tists alike today believe, a thought in the Mind of God that
> brought it—and the entire universe itself—into existence?*

But there's more: The Coma-Virgo Cluster is now
known to be part of a much vaster *supercluster of galaxies!* I'm reminded here of the famed "Deep-Field" images
taken by the Hubble Space Telescope (and available for
viewing on its website). In one of them, this amazing instrument was pointed at a piece of sky the size of a grain
of sand held at arm's length. For 100 hours as the Hubble
orbited the Earth at nearly 18,000 miles per hour (that's
5 miles per second), it not only was kept pointed at that
tiny spot but continually "photographed" it. (What an
astounding technological achievement!) When the final
image was released, it showed *over 10,000 galaxies in that
sand-grain speck of sky!*

I remember hearing a rabbi once say that there's only one kind of real prayer. It's when you see something so amazing, so magnificent, that it leaves you speechless and in awe. I believe that a universe filled with endless numbers of galaxies eminently qualifies. Indeed, aren't the graceful, spinning spiral galaxies themselves celestial "prayer-wheels"?

Colliding Galaxies

As I pointed out in Chapter 14, stars never actually collide (some close binary stars do coalesce but not "collide"), due to the vast distances between them in comparison to their physical sizes. But galaxies are another matter! With so many of them—especially in crowded clusters, like the Coma-Virgo swarm—and given their colossal sizes, they do occasionally collide. However, this is not like two freight trains smashing into each other. Galaxies do everything with grace! When they slowly merge together, they pass through each other like phantoms in the night. The stars in them are unaffected, but the gas and dust do energetically interact, resulting in a new wave of star birth in both systems. Some of these interacting galaxies as revealed in Hubble images actually look just like human embryos!

There is one pair of colliding galaxies that's a fascinating sight in binoculars. Known as the *Black Belt Galaxy,* from a rim of dark material circling its apparent equator, this object was long thought to be an edge-on galaxy like the Sombrero. But more recent optical and radio imaging has proved it to be a pair of supermassive galaxies embracing each other! And it's a relatively easy find despite being low in the spring sky as seen from mid-northern latitudes in the southern constellation of Centaurus. It lies due south of the bright star Spica in Virgo—and about five degrees north of the magnificent globular star cluster Omega Centauri, described in Chapter 14.

The Black Belt is fully three times as large as the Milky Way in actual size! Its appearance in a small telescope has been described as like the two halves of a broken egg. At a distance of 22.5 million light-years, it's one of the nearest colliding galaxies. The next-brightest one is nearly four magnitudes fainter (and also four times as remote), so the Black Belt Galaxy reigns supreme as the finest example of these galactic mergers in the heavens for viewing by stargazers.

Quasars

Imagine a tiny blue point of light in the sky—one having the luminosity of *all the stars in its parent galaxy combined!* That's a *quasar* (the name being derived from "quasi-stellar" object or source). They are the brightest objects in the cosmos, along with supernova explosions (and *gamma-ray bursts,* thought to be the merger of two black holes!). And because they are so brilliant, they can be seen all the way to the edge of the observable universe—out to nearly 14 billion light-years! They are thought to be the bright centers of distant galaxies where matter is falling into the massive black holes that appear to reside at their hearts.

The brightest and closest quasar to us is located in the spring constellation Virgo and goes by the nondescript designation "3C-273." Surprisingly, no one has ever come up with a popular name for this hugely significant and important object. In my personal list of celestial targets for viewing, I simply refer to it as "First Quasar." Not very creative on my part either! But I was the first person to ever write an article on actually *looking* at quasars with backyard telescopes (which appeared in the December 1979 issue of *Astronomy* magazine). Up until then no one, it seems, had thought about looking upon one of these beasts in anything other than huge observatory instruments.

Although it's the closest of its kind to us, this quasar is still some two billion light-years away! And I'll tell you how to locate it. But first, let me be up-front with you. You can't see it with the unaided eye, binoculars no matter how big, a spotting scope, or even a small telescope. You need at least a 6-inch glass (it has actually been glimpsed in a 4-inch by some eagle-eyed observers) and lots of experience at locating deep-space objects in order to succeed. But it's worth any effort to get its archaic photons in your eye! As stargazer Peter Lord puts it: "Time spent with two-billion-year-old photons is potent stuff."

One solution is to attend a spring star party at your local astronomy club—and ask the proud owner of some big scope there to show you 3C-273. In case he or she doesn't know where it is, here's how to find it: First locate the 3rd-magnitude star Porrima (Gamma Virginia) to the upper right (northwest) of bright blue-white Spica. (These are the same two stars used to locate the Sombrero Galaxy.) To the right (west) of Porrima is a fainter star—Eta Virginis. 3C-273 lies to the north and precisely at the corner of a right triangle formed with these two stars. Sweeping that spot, look for a very dim bluish-appearing "star." The quasar itself is actually easier to see at some times than at others, as it varies in brightness by about a magnitude irregularly over time.

Meditative Moment

Although it's not really much to look at visually, when 3C-273's baffling nature and significance in the cosmic scheme of things is appreciated, catching sight of this quasar is a thrilling experience (as those who have seen it, myself included, will verify). To think that the light we see coming from it tonight left there when single-celled life-forms ruled the Earth! This sends chills up my spine whenever I contemplate it. (And sometimes tears to my eyes, for reasons I'm at a loss to explain.)

It's nothing less than amazing to me that a small disk of optical glass can capture and bring into focus those ancient photons of light from this remote object that have traversed the expanse of the visible universe on a journey lasting billions of years. Truly, the telescope is a wonderful magic "time machine" that makes possible heady explorations of creation at the simple turn of a knob!

No End in Sight!

So we've now come to the end of our travelogue, having sampled some of the sky's visual treasures for the spiritually minded stargazer. These have ranged from gloriously thrilling sights to challenging ghostly glows at the limits of vision. (Regarding these latter dim objects, a line from the poem "In Evening Air" by

Theodore Roethke always comes to mind: "Ye littles, lie more close!")

We've found that the farther out you go into this amazing universe, the fainter things become—but also the more significant in the grand hierarchy of the cosmos itself. However, it is my earnest wish that you never cease touring the wonders of the heavens, for truly "the sky's the limit!"

••••• **CHAPTER 18** •••••

CELEBRATING THE UNIVERSE!

Poet and priest Gerard Manley Hopkins (whom I quoted in Chapter 3) once exclaimed, "What I do is me: for that I came!" The late visionary and writer Ray Bradbury often said that *he* came "to celebrate the universe," which he did superbly using his lifelong love affair with words and metaphors.

As for myself, I definitely came to this planet to celebrate the magnificence of the universe—a universe from which we sprang and to which we are destined to return! As Wayne Dyer urges in his wonderful Hay House movie *The Shift,* "Don't die with your music still inside of you." I can honestly say that this is my "music."

In this final chapter, I'd like to offer some inspiration for your continuing journey, with ideas for how you might unleash *your* music and celebrate the universe, following the example of other fellow stargazers.

Modes of Celebration

I've been sharing my passion for stargazing ever since I was a teenager with as many people as possible through writing, speaking, teaching, and viewing the sky (all of which I've been actively doing since the age of 12). I've also spent lots of time on street corners—no, not loitering, but *stargazing!* This has been as part of the nationwide "sidewalk astronomy" movement started by former monk and telescope-making guru John Dobson (for whom the popular Dobsonian telescope mounting is named). Many amateur astronomers regularly share their telescopes and binoculars with passersby on city streets across the U.S., spreading their love for the universe to countless others.

Hopefully, you will personally join in the celebration, in whatever way you feel led, as a result of having read this celestial travel guide. No, it doesn't have to be in such dramatic public fashion as what the sidewalk astronomers do (which does take some courage, depending on your personality!). Participating as a group in a scheduled astronomy-club star party is much less "scary" to those who are on the shy side. These are typically held in city or county or even national parks rather than on busy street corners.

And indeed, many stargazers prefer to do their celebrating alone in contemplative silence in the privacy of their own backyard. But even here, don't overlook the importance of sharing the sky with others whenever opportunities happen to present themselves. To touch even one person's life this way can have a wonderful and profound impact on them (and potentially on our world as well). In any case, the universe openly welcomes all who celebrate its magnificence in whatever way they choose!

The Great Disconnect

This section is for those readers who already own (or plan to someday obtain) a telescope. The same technology that has revolutionized professional astronomy today is being used by many stargazers to automatically point their telescopes and make observations of celestial objects using video and CCD cameras—all from the comfort of their living rooms or dens! To us "purists," this loses much of the charm of stargazing and defeats its real purpose: to commune one-on-one *directly* with the living universe—not a cold image or reproduction of it. (As one traditionalist points out: "Looking at an image of a celestial object on a computer screen is like looking at a photo of your wife when she is standing right beside you." And yet another adds: "I would rather freeze or fight off mosquitoes than play astronomy on a computer.")

Recall the amazing "photon connection" discussed in Chapter 3 (that the dualistic wave-particles streaming in from space from celestial objects *were once inside of them and are now in contact with your retinas!*). Only by actually *looking* at the universe with your own eyes and soaking up archaic photons from across space and time can you be physically and intimately connected to it. It's the old story of seeing a photograph of Saturn (however spectacular it may be) as opposed to glimpsing the real thing "live" (no matter how small the image may appear in backyard scopes). There's simply no comparison.

But everything has its place, and balance is certainly key here, as in other endeavors. However you choose to stargaze, make sure that you spend at least some time actually "gazing" at your targets! It's one of the benefits of naked-eye observing that you do have to explore the sky using nothing more than your own eyes. But with or without optical aid, looking skyward is always a sublime way to spend a starry night.

Starlight Nights

One stargazer whose entire "career" in astronomy was strictly that of a visual observer was Leslie Peltier. He spent most of his life on a farm in Ohio, sweeping the skies for new comets (he found 12 of them!) and making scientifically valuable observations of the brightness of variable stars (more than 130,000 of them!) from his two backyard observatories. He also discovered six novae with his unaided eye alone. Harlow Shapley, onetime director of the Harvard College Observatory, called him "the world's greatest nonprofessional astronomer."

Despite being offered paid staff positions at several major observatories, Peltier preferred instead to stargaze from his farm. He was a shy, retiring man of introspective depth who loved his home so much that he rarely ever left it—even to receive awards honoring him at astronomical conferences.

I visited him on two occasions, and reviewed his autobiography *Starlight Nights: The Adventures of a Star-Gazer* for *Sky & Telescope* magazine when it was first released in 1965. For 70 years he "celebrated the universe" as few ever have, from first sighting Halley's Comet as a child in 1910 until his death in 1980. There's something he said that I very much want to share with you as a fellow stargazer—something quaint and simple, but also very profound:

> Were I to write out one prescription designed to help alleviate at least some of the self-made miseries of mankind, it would read like this: One gentle dose of starlight to be taken each clear night just before retiring.

Sage advice from one of the greatest stargazers of all time. (His autobiography is recommended reading for anyone who loves the stars. It will take you back to a simpler, saner era that many have referred to as the "golden age" of astronomy. It's available from **www .shopatsky.com**.)

The Man Who Loved the Stars

And now here's the story of another, earlier stargazer (in this case, one that illustrates just how far an exalted love of the stars can propel an individual)—famed telescope maker and astronomy popularizer John Alfred Brashear, whom I mentioned in Chapter 4.

Having only a third-grade education, he spent his early years working in the steel mills of Pittsburgh as a millwright. He loved looking at the stars from the cinder piles near the river on Saturday nights when the mill shut down and the smoky sky cleared. Longing to have a telescope of his own, he taught himself how to grind and polish lenses and mirrors, and in time became perhaps the greatest lens maker of his day. His optical genius attracted the attention of several of the city's philanthropists, who set him up in business—leading to the construction of some of the largest research telescopes in the world at that time (a number of which are still in active use today). Brashear also made many smaller instruments for schools and colleges and even for private individuals.

In the later years of his life, he served as acting director of the new Allegheny Observatory (for which he raised the construction funds) and acting chancellor of the University of Pittsburgh, and was the moving force behind the founding of Carnegie Technical Institute (now Carnegie Mellon University). He was widely admired and honored both at home and abroad—not only for his telescope-making feats, but also for his inspired lectures about the heavens to people of all ages and backgrounds.

At the time of his death in 1920, he had more than *two dozen* honorary degrees bestowed upon him! And all of this from a man of humble origins, spurred on by a passionate love affair with the stars and a desire to share it with everyone he met. Brashear's ashes were mixed with those of his wife (who played a major role in his success) and placed in a crypt in the base of one of the two big research telescopes built by his company at the Allegheny Observatory. A plague attached to the crypt reads: WE HAVE LOVED THE STARS TOO FONDLY TO BE FEARFUL OF THE NIGHT.

And here I recall these words from naturalist John Burroughs: "But to know is not all, it is only half; to love is the other half." Hopefully by now you *have* fallen in love with the universe on our cosmic journey. Most astronomers I know—both amateur and professional—have a "love affair" with it, which increasing knowledge of its wonders over time only deepens. They are firmly convinced that the universe loves them in return. May it be so for you as well!

AFTERWORD

Final Thoughts

In Fyodor Dostoyevsky's *The Brothers Karamazov,* one of the lead characters, Alyosha, is described as being in rapture over the stars "shining at him from across the abyss of space"—and actually weeping unashamedly in his ecstasy. Talk about celebrating the universe! Alyosha also felt that there were "threads from all those innumerable worlds of God, linking his soul to them"—talk about being connected to the universe!

Looking upon the magnificence of the heavens in childlike wonder and awe as a stargazer is surely a superb way to celebrate it. Emerson talked about the stars pouring out "their almost spiritual rays" upon us, and of a human becoming like a child under their influence. Indeed, gazing into a timeless universe and the beginning of everything, we feel ourselves become young once again. The night sky is a portal to transcendence from the shackles and concerns of adulthood, freeing the child within us to play under the stars.

The scientific revelations of modern astronomy and cosmology provide the basis for the universe's wonder. But it's the metaphysics and spirituality and aesthetics of the heavens that make it truly meaningful and personal to each individual.

Our celestial voyage in this book has been first and foremost a spiritual pilgrimage into the very soul of the night. It's been a quest to personally experience and commune with that awesome Power behind all of creation, as pinnacled in the starry heavens above. This was simply and beautifully expressed by the great Henry David Thoreau when he said that one of his earliest memories was of "looking through the stars to see if I could see God behind them."

That's really what you and I have been doing throughout these pages. We've learned that our very bodies are made of stardust. We've meditated upon the stars—and actually touched them through the amazing photon connection, in which part of them has entered our eyes and expanded our consciousness. We've sensed the immensity of time and space, seen the wondrous beauty of the firmament, and marveled at the divine order evident everywhere we've looked. I believe that we have, indeed, seen and felt God in looking at and through the stars!

We have roamed far and wide on our cosmic journey—beginning here on our beautiful Planet Earth and ending up at the very edge of the observable universe. We've seen wonders enough for a lifetime. At every turn there have been sights that few except star lovers even dream about, let alone see. And yet, as I stated in the Introduction, the cosmic journey is a never-ending one.

If it's clear tonight, I'll venture out under the stars and renew acquaintances with many "old friends" in the sky. But I will also most assuredly see wonders completely new to me. And this comes after a lifetime of combing the heavens for its treasures from a purely aesthetic point of view. My close, personal encounter with the universe will continue to grow, as I hope yours will as well.

Observing seems so natural, so real, so compelling. How could it be otherwise? The heavens feed us—first the body, then the mind, and then the soul. *How can we possibly not embrace and love and celebrate the universe?*

My parting fond wish for you is that you will find stargazing a thrilling adventure, and a source of joy and inspiration, always. Until we meet again (perhaps in the cosmic corridors "out there"), keep looking up!

APPENDIX A

Stargazing Resources

To make your cosmic journey more enjoyable and meaningful, listed here are a few of the amazing multitude of aids available to today's stargazer. Of necessity, I've limited this selection to some of my favorites. While many of these have been mentioned in the text itself, they are being listed here all in one place for convenient reference.

Popular-Level Magazines

Sky & Telescope (**www.skyandtelescope.com**)

Astronomy (**www.astronomy.com**)

Popular-Level Books

Stars, by H. Zim, R. Baker, and M. Chartrand, New York: Golden Books Publishing Company (finest introductory guide to the heavens ever written, for readers of all ages!)

NightWatch: A Practical Guide to Observing the Universe, by T. Dickinson, Buffalo, NY: Firefly Books

Classic Astronomy Books

(most out of print, but available in libraries, used bookstores, and on the Internet)

The Friendly Stars, by M. E. Martin, New York: Dover Publications

Field Book of the Skies, by W. T. Olcott, New York: G.P. Putnam's Sons

1001 Celestial Wonders, by C. E. Barns, Morgan Hill, CA: Pacific Science Press (self-published)

New Handbook of the Heavens, by H. Bernhard, D. Bennett, and H. Rice, New York: McGraw-Hill (my all-time favorite stargazing book!)

Starlight Nights, by L. Peltier, Cambridge, MA: Sky Publishing Corporation (still in print)

Star Maps, Star Atlases & Rotating Star Charts

Sky Publishing Corporation (**www.ShopatSky.com**)

Edmund Scientifics (**www.scientificsonline.com**)

The Stars: A New Way to See Them, by H. A. Rey, Boston: Houghton Mifflin (this delightful volume is available in most bookstores and on Amazon; to see it, go to the following site: **http://www.codex99.com/ illustration/26.html**)

Find the Constellations, by H. A. Rey, Boston: Houghton Mifflin (companion volume to above)

Lunar/Planetary Maps & Globes

Sky Publishing Corporation (**www.shopatsky.com**)

U.S. Geological Survey (**www.mapaplanet.org**)

Telescopes, Binoculars & Accessories

Orion Telescopes & Binoculars (**www.oriontelescopes.com**)

Edmund Scientifics (**www.scientificsonline.com**)

Celestron (**www.celestron.com**)

A Buyer's and User's Guide to Astronomical Telescopes & Binoculars, by J. Mullaney, New York: Springer (**www.springer.com**)

Satellite-Tracking Sites

Real Time Satellite Tracking (**www.n2yo.com**)

Heavens Above (**www.heavens-above.com**)

NASA (**www.J-Pass.com**)

Apps for Identifying Planets, Stars, Constellations & Much More

Sky Map

Star Walk

Pocket Universe

Luminos

GoSkyWatch Planetarium

Starmap HD

(all available from iTunes: **www.itunes.com**)

The finest and most comprehensive listing of the (somewhat overwhelming) multitude of astronomy-related apps is compiled by the American Astronomical Society, which provides brief descriptions of each and websites at the following lengthy URL: **http://scitation.aip.org/getpdf/servlet/GetPDFServlet?filetype=pdf&id=AERSCZ000010000001010302000001&idtype=cvips&doi=10.3847/AER2011036&prog=normaldun**

Celestial/Space Music

The Stargazer's Journey (among many other related albums), by Jonn Serrie (available from **www.thousandstar.com** or Amazon)

Best of the Pleiades, by Gerald Jay Markoe (available from CD Universe: **www.cduniverse.com**)

Theme from the *Cosmos* PBS television series—*Heaven and Hell* (Movement 3), by Vangelis (available from: **www.vangelismovements.com/heavenandhell**)

The Planets (Venus, Saturn, Uranus, and Neptune cuts), by Gustav Holst (widely available in music stores and on numerous websites)

Astronomical Societies

The Astronomical League (**www.astroleague.org**)

Astronomical Society of the Pacific (**http://astrosociety.org**)

International Dark-Sky Association (**www.darksky.org**)

The Planetary Society (**www.planetary.org**)

. . . plus local astronomy clubs for most cities, as listed on *Sky & Telescope*'s website (see above)

Space Images

Hubble Space Telescope (**www.hubblesite.org**)

Astronomy Picture of the Day (**http://apod.nasa.gov/ apod/astropix.html**)

Miscellaneous

Cosmos, by Carl Sagan, New York: Random House (DVD of the 13-part PBS series available from Amazon)

The Carl Sagan Portal (**www.carlsagan.com**)

Radical Amazement, by J. Cannato, Notre Dame, IN: Sorin Books

The Journey to Palomar, DVD (inspiring account of George Ellery Hale's vision for building four of the world's largest telescopes, culminating in Palomar—and for whom its 200-inch Hale telescope is named; this documentary, hailed as a "journey of the spirit," is available from PBS: **www.shoppbs.org**)

APPENDIX B

Top Dozen "Must-See" Celestial Showpieces

Here's my recommended "bucket list" for beginning stargazers. For the first four entries, consult *Sky & Telescope* or *Astronomy* magazine for dates and times of visibility. Host constellation and season best seen are given for the remainder. (The four objects shown in brackets are for Southern Hemisphere stargazers, as "replacements" for the objects above them—which can't be seen from there.) Enjoy!

1. Total Eclipse of the Sun

2. Total Eclipse of the Moon

3. Jupiter & Its Satellites

4. Saturn & Its Rings

5. Star Sirius* (Canis Major—winter)

6. Pleiades Star Cluster (Taurus—winter)

7. Orion Nebula & Trapezium (Orion—winter)

8. Beehive Star Cluster (Cancer—spring) [Jewel Box Cluster/Southern Cross (Crux— spring)]

9. Double Star Albireo (Cygnus—summer/fall) [Double Star Alpha Centauri (Centaurus— spring)]

10. Hercules Star Cluster (Hercules—summer) [Omega Centauri Cluster (Centaurus— spring)]

11. Milky Way Galaxy (all-sky—fall/summer)

12. Andromeda Galaxy (Andromeda—fall) [Large Magellanic Cloud (Dorado—year- round)]

*Brightest of the heavenly host—a dazzling bluish-white diamond!

ACKNOWLEDGMENTS

It's my sincere pleasure to thank my kind and patient editor at Hay House, Alex Freemon, whose masterful input has so greatly enhanced the manuscript of this labor-of-love. I am also deeply grateful to Louise Hay, the beloved founder of Hay House, and to Reid Tracy, president and CEO, for their vision in publishing this unique spiritual-scientific guide to personally experiencing the wonders of our awesome universe. Special recognition and heartfelt thanks to dear friends Warren and Marge Greenwald, who have long encouraged me in my mission of "celestial evangelism" and believed in the need for an inspirational work on this subject. Finally, while I've already dedicated this book to my wife, Sharon, I must again recognize her contributions by saying that my debt of gratitude for all she has done is quite beyond expression. I spent years "searching the heavens" for her—when in fact she was right here, close by, on Planet Earth all along!

ABOUT THE AUTHOR

James Mullaney is an astronomy writer and speaker who has published nearly a thousand articles and nine books on observing the wonders of the heavens and logged over 20,000 hours of stargazing time with the unaided eye, binoculars, and telescopes. Formerly Curator of the Buhl Planetarium & Institute of Popular Science in Pittsburgh and Director of the University of South Carolina's DuPont Planetarium, Jim served as staff astronomer at the University of Pittsburgh's Allegheny Observatory and as an editor for *Sky & Telescope* magazine. One of the contributors to Carl Sagan's acclaimed *Cosmos* PBS television series, he has received recognition over the years from such notables (and fellow stargazers) as Sir Arthur Clarke, Johnny Carson, Ray Bradbury, Dr. Wernher von Braun, and his former student retired NASA scientist/astronaut Dr. Jay Apt.

Jim's lifelong mission has been to "celebrate the universe!"—to get others to look up at the majesty of the night sky and personally experience the joys of stargazing. It's estimated that more than a million people of all ages, faiths, and backgrounds have heard his inspiring messages. In recognition of his work, he has been elected a Fellow of the prestigious Royal Astronomical Society of London.

Hay House Titles of Related Interest

YOU CAN HEAL YOUR LIFE, the movie,
starring Louise L. Hay & Friends
(available as a 1-DVD program and an expanded 2-DVD set)
Watch the trailer at: **www.LouiseHayMovie.com**

THE SHIFT, the movie,
starring Dr. Wayne W. Dyer
(available as a 1-DVD program and an expanded 2-DVD set)
Watch the trailer at: **www.DyerMovie.com**

CosMos: A Co-creator's Guide to the Whole-World,
by Ervin Laszlo and Jude Currivan

*THE DIVINE MATRIX: Bridging Time, Space, Miracles,
and Belief,* by Gregg Braden

*THE HONEYMOON EFFECT: The Science of Creating
Heaven on Earth,* by Bruce H. Lipton, Ph.D.

THE HOPE: A Guide to Sacred Activism, by Andrew Harvey

NATURE'S SECRET MESSAGES: Hidden in Plain Sight,
by Elaine Wilkes

QUANTUM CREATIVITY: Think Quantum, Be Creative,
by Amit Goswami, Ph.D.

WISHES FULFILLED: Mastering the Art of Manifesting,
by Dr. Wayne W. Dyer

All of the above are available at your
local bookstore, or may be ordered by visiting:

Hay House USA: **www.hayhouse.com**®
Hay House Australia: **www.hayhouse.com.au**
Hay House UK: **www.hayhouse.co.uk**
Hay House South Africa: **www.hayhouse.co.za**
Hay House India: **www.hayhouse.co.in**

We hope you enjoyed this Hay House book. If you'd like
to receive our online catalog featuring additional information
on Hay House books and products, or if you'd like to find
out more about the Hay Foundation, please contact:

Hay House, Inc., P.O. Box 5100, Carlsbad, CA 92018-5100
(760) 431-7695 or (800) 654-5126
(760) 431-6948 (fax) or (800) 650-5115 (fax)
www.hayhouse.com® • **www.hayfoundation.org**

Published and distributed in Australia by: Hay House Australia Pty.
Ltd., 18/36 Ralph St., Alexandria NSW 2015 • *Phone:* 612-9669-4299
• *Fax:* 612-9669-4144 • www.hayhouse.com.au

Published and distributed in the United Kingdom by:
Hay House UK, Ltd., Astley House, 33 Notting Hill Gate, London
W11 3JQ • *Phone:* 44-20-3675-2450 • *Fax:* 44-20-3675-2451
www.hayhouse.co.uk

Published and distributed in the Republic of South Africa by:
Hay House SA (Pty), Ltd., P.O. Box 990, Witkoppen 2068
Phone/Fax: 27-11-467-8904 • www.hayhouse.co.za

Published in India by: Hay House Publishers India, Muskaan
Complex, Plot No. 3, B-2, Vasant Kunj, New Delhi 110 070 • *Phone:*
91-11-4176-1620 • *Fax:* 91-11-4176-1630 • www.hayhouse.co.in

Distributed in Canada by: Raincoast, 9050 Shaughnessy St.,
Vancouver, B.C. V6P 6E5 • *Phone:* (604) 323-7100
Fax: (604) 323-2600 • www.raincoast.com

Take Your Soul on a Vacation

Visit **www.HealYourLife.com®** to regroup, recharge,
and reconnect with your own magnificence.
Featuring blogs, mind-body-spirit news, and life-changing
wisdom from Louise Hay and friends.

Visit **www.HealYourLife.com** today!